# EVERY BELIEVER'S GUIDE TO THE
# SUPERNATURAL

*EXPERIENCING HEAVEN'S RAIN*

❧ P.L. Shang ❧

---

**DESTINY IMAGE EUROPE**™ **srl**
**Via Maiella, 1**
**66020 San Giovanni Teatino (Ch) - Italy**

*"Changing the world, one book at a time."*

This book and all other Destiny Image Europe™ books are available at Christian bookstores and distributors worldwide.

To order products, or for any other correspondence, please contact:

**DESTINY IMAGE EUROPE**™ **srl**
Via Acquacorrente, 6
65123 - Pescara - Italy
Tel. +39 085 4716623 - Fax: +39 085 4716622
E-mail: info@eurodestinyimage.com

Or reach us on the Internet: **www.eurodestinyimage.com**

---

ISBN-13: 978-88-89127-51-3

*For Worldwide Distribution, Printed in Italy.*

1 2 3 4 5 6 7 8/10 09 08 07

# Dedication

Dedicated to God, my heavenly Father; Jesus Christ, my Lord and Savior; and Holy Spirit, my Friend, Guide, and Teacher.

# *Acknowledgments*

I never thought I would see this day come. Soon after writing this book in May 2006, God arranged a divine connection with Destiny Image Europe in early 2007. Although this book is my life story, the penmanship belongs to the Holy Spirit, and I cannot claim any credit for its birth. May all the glory go to God, my heavenly Father—thank You for being an amazing Father to me. To Jesus Christ, my Lord and Savior—thank You for dying on the cross for my sins, and in exchange, I give you all that is mine while receiving all that is Yours. To the Holy Spirit, my Friend and Counselor—thank You for Your revelations, for Your comfort, and for Your gentle promptings and leadings.

I would like to take this opportunity to thank my earthly parents for giving birth to me; without them I would have no story to speak of. I want to especially thank my sister Pei. You are the best sister in the whole world, and I wouldn't want any other sister than you. You have been so generous and supportive to me even when you did not understand what God was doing in my life, and you stood beside me during all the storms. Our family owes you a debt that we cannot repay, and I ask our heavenly Father to ensure that His blessings overflow in your life. In addition, I want to thank you, my brother and my deceased sister, for also being part of my life.

I would like to thank everyone at Destiny Image Europe for making this book a possibility. Thank you for your vision to seek out and publish fresh God-given messages written by brothers and sisters from all over the world, whether famous or unknown. I want to especially thank Pietro Evangelista, the publisher, for his telephone call that gave me the courage to take a step of faith to publish this book. Your encouragement, assurance, and dedication for the sake of the Kingdom are much appreciated.

I would also especially like to thank a few special people who have been a great source of encouragement to me. Your presence in my life has made a significant difference! Kit, thank you for sharing with me your DTS YWAM experience (Discipleship Training School through Youth With a Mission) that planted a desire in my heart to also complete this course, which eventually led to an adventure that transformed my life and allowed me to encounter God face-to-face. Thank you for your suggestions, input, and legal advice as well as the encouragement to trust God and live by faith as I pursued publishing this book. Thank you for believing in me. I appreciate your friendship.

Angeline, I thank God for you. Your presence in my life during these past few years has been a godsend. I appreciate the times we have spent together praying and believing God even when the external physical circumstances did not correspond to our belief of the goodness of our Abba Father. Let's continue to believe and trust, and with eyes of faith we will see God move even more powerfully in the years to come.

Mariette, thank you for all the impartation during my DTS. I learned and gained so much from your wisdom, your teaching, your love, care, and concern. Thank you for your spiritual leadership and parenting even though it was for such a short period of my life. You made an impact and personal difference during that amazing season. I deeply appreciate all that you did.

Finally, I thank all my friends who stood with me in prayer—Victor, May, Reinske, Tim, Ghani, Monica, and many others. I appreciate your prayers. Thank you for believing in me!

# *Endorsement*

P. L. writes from her heart as she shares her spiritual journey with us. And hidden within her experiences and encounters are nuggets of truth that will outlast the tenure of her own life. Read this book from the perspective of a fellow traveller on a spiritual journey and you will glean much from it. I commend this book to you enthusiastically.

*Benny Ho,* Senior Pastor
Faith Community Church
Perth, Western Australia
Founder, Arrows School of Ministry

# Table of Contents

# Introduction

I have asked myself many times, what is my purpose for writing this book about my life? Is anyone ever going to publish it? Even if someone does publish it, will anyone buy it?

I believe I am writing this book, first of all, because the Holy Spirit wants me to write this book about my life. Thus, writing is an act of obedience to what God has called me to do. Secondly, I am writing this book for me—as a reminder of God's goodness in my life, and as a dedication to Him and for what He has done in my life ever since I took that first step of faith to accept Jesus Christ as my personal Lord and Savior. Lastly, I am writing this book for all the lay members of the Church body—those who are not pastors, preachers, missionaries, or evangelists. This book is written by one of you for you because I want to affirm that what the Bible says is true—all of us are part of the Body of Christ, and we all have a purpose in His Kingdom.

Some of us might go on to do great exploits for God and become well-known throughout the Church world, while many others will remain faceless and nameless in many aspects; but this does not determine the significance of our existence during such a time as this. We all are privileged to be called to live in these last days during which the coming of our Lord Jesus is becoming more and more obvious according to the signs happening around us, as was prophesied so many years ago. All of us as believers have a part to play in the coming Kingdom, and no role is too small.

However, many of us feel small, insignificant, and powerless, and have been praying many years for spiritual advancement in our own lives as well as in the churches we attend. Moreover, many of us are weary and tired. Although we continue to cry out to God, we have yet to see a breakthrough. Perhaps we have waited for five, ten, or even twenty years, but we have not experienced the success we desire.

I am writing this book to tell you that something will happen—someday, somehow. God hears every prayer of every one of His children. Not one prayer remains unheard. And one day, in His time, He will come in His majesty and sweep you and me off our feet; therefore, we must not give up even if the going is tough. God has never promised that there would be no rain, but He has promised that He will be with us when it does rain.

So, I urge you, brothers and sisters, to not give up, to go on believing in God, and to keep on praying even if the external physical circumstances appear to be at a standstill. Remember that there is a war occurring in the spiritual realm, and although God might be delayed, He will definitely come (see Dan. 10:12-14). Don't stop one prayer short of the miracle.

Your very next prayer might be the prayer to bring the miracle into your life. Perhaps you will soon move from Marah to Elim (see Exod. 15:22-27). Sometimes you might not even be aware of your success until it is over, and like Jacob you will proclaim, "Surely the Lord is in this place; and I knew it not" (Gen. 28:16b).

May we all continue to look forward to what is ahead of us and to work out our salvation with fear and trembling (see Phil. 2:12), because surely He who promises is faithful, and all that He promises will come to pass. Heaven and earth will pass away, but not one of His words will pass away (see Matt. 24:35).

Instead of hearing about all the adventures, miracles, signs, and wonders that other people have experienced, let's go on an adventure ourselves. Let's ask God to come and move in our land and bring us to the place where we are living in the supernatural and unexplainable ways of God. Oftentimes, it might seem hard, depressing, and difficult; many people will misunderstand you, your heart, or your intentions; but God will not. He will always be there, and He will always stand beside you. God knows and sees us in our weakness and in our inability; He has never had any illusions about us. Scripture tells us that when we are weak, we will be made strong (see 2 Cor. 12:10). Our strength is not in ourselves but in the living God.

One day, He will turn up in your life, just as He did in mine, and you will be forever ruined for the ordinary because you will have had a small glimpse of His true nature and what He is like. You will know His goodness, and you will hold on to His hand and trust. "Trust in the Lord with all thine heart; and lean not unto thine own understanding. In all thy ways acknowledge Him, and He shall direct thy paths" (Prov. 3:5-6). I pray that God will deposit His Spirit in you even as you read this book, that He will speak tenderly to you and allow you to have a glimpse of Him that will change your life, that after reading this book, your eyes will be renewed with faith to believe that God will come through in your circumstances. As Graham Cooke says, we all must learn to see God in our life, in the ebb and in the flow, when He manifests Himself and His presence, when He hides Himself, when He is there to our senses, and when He is not there.

P.L. Shang

## CHAPTER ONE

# *This Was My Life*

Jesus suffered and *His scars are mementoes* of the pain He endured for us. Remember that your scars may be your greatest ministry.[1]

Adrian Rogers

*All we like sheep have gone astray; we have turned every one to his own way; and the Lord hath laid on Him the iniquity of us all* (Isaiah 53:6).

## *A Superstitious Beginning*

L
ike many Singaporeans, I grew up in a non-Christian home. My family was heavily involved in idol worship and ancestor worship. Among my grandparents and parents, we owned about 20 man-made idols at home,

including the "earth god," "sky god," and "guan yin"; and we visited the temples often. We would participate in huge celebrations during the "Seventh Month," otherwise known as the "Ghost Festival," and we would prepare much food and incense on such days. We also celebrated the "Qing Ming" festival when the dead are remembered and invited to dine at home. Tables would be laid with food, and furniture would be set in place to welcome the dead relatives or the gods, depending on the festivals we were celebrating that day. There was daily burning of incense and joss sticks and annual celebrations, as well as monthly full moon celebrations.

My father had many good friends who were mediums, and we were often involved in spiritual rituals where these mediums would invite the gods to possess them and manifest themselves as "monkey gods." Once possessed, they would perform feats like eating fire and carrying extremely heavy weights. My father was superstitious to the extent that when his children fell sick, he would not take us to the doctors but would write words on the talisman, burn it, put it in water, and give it to us to drink as our healing remedy.

I was very young when my grandfather died. But even though I was a youngster at the time, I can still remember the death funeral vividly. There was a huge celebration, and many people came to pay their last respects to him. A tent was set up in which his coffin was placed. Daily, people would come to visit, and nightly, tables full of people would play mahjong. There was much feasting and merrymaking during the five-day wake.

But what actually held my curiosity as a very young child were the rituals that were performed during the funeral. Taoist priests came in their robes and used many gadgets for these nightly rituals that lasted for a few hours. They would chant for a long time, and they would sing funny songs that no one seemed to understand. Then they would perform all kinds of rituals where they would hold the lantern in front of an animal, such as a duck or a chicken, and lead it to walk across a small paper bridge. This act symbolized the crossing of the dead to the nether world or realm. Then there would be breaking of bricks and many other acts that would be performed during the funeral rites. The noise and the rituals would continue daily until the body was cremated.

And so, my life was seeped with superstition, rites, and rituals for many years until I gave my life to the Lord Jesus Christ and accepted Him as my personal Lord and Savior.

## Generational Curses

I grew up knowing that my family was different. Life was not easy even as a young child. For instance, when I was very young, I knew that my mom was schizophrenic (mental illness), and I had a hard time accepting it. Throughout my growing years, I felt it was a stigma and a shame, and I never told any of my friends, even people whom I knew very well, about her illness. I assumed that people would think that if my mom was schizophrenic, I would be schizophrenic as well; and I feared their rejection. And so, I kept this secret and never revealed it to anyone. It was not until my early 20's when my mother's condition was much more stable and she was no longer in and out of the mental institution that I began to share much more openly about my family background. I had no idea then that there was a generational curse upon my family. My mom's aunt as well as my eldest sister suffered from schizophrenia. Thus, there are already three generations who have been cursed. Only later did I understand this curse and was able to break its poison from my family line.

Then in my late 20's, when I moved from a traditional church to a charismatic church, I was taught about sin and generational curses, and gained a better understanding of the curses that afflicted my own family tree. Part of the curses included the premature death of my uncle who drowned at sea when he was 16 years old and an aunt who committed suicide in her early 20's. Derek Prince's excellent book, *Blessings and Curses, You Can Choose*[2] was a godsend that one of my spiritual mentors advised me to read when she found out about my family history. In this book, Prince expounds much with regard to the causes of curses in a person's life and the indications that could signal the existence of a curse, as well as the divine exchange that was made on the cross by Jesus Christ and how to be released from the curse.

## The Pain of Rejection

While I was growing up, my father was often not at home, and it was my grandmother who literally raised me, my two sisters, and my brother. My father would often drink, gamble, and participate in activities outside the family. Because my two siblings and I, birthed by my mother, were all girls, my father had another woman. In the Chinese tradition, only sons become heirs of the family and are considered able to carry the family bloodline. Daughters, once married, change their surname to that of their husbands and hence belong to the husband's family. In my father's sight, daughters were unable to carry on his bloodline and would one day leave home. Therefore, he desperately wanted a son. My half brother of the same father but different mother was born three months after I was born.

It was years later, when I was in my late 20's, that God revealed to me that I was rejected at birth because I was born a girl and not a boy. Shortly after I realized this fact, I was heart-broken, but God in His grace and mercy allowed me to attend a sermon that brought life and understanding to my soul. God's Word gave me comfort and assured me that when my father and mother forsake or reject me, then the Lord will take care of me (see Ps. 27:10). I came to understand that rejection prevents us from enjoying God totally. Satan faced rejection when he sinned against God and was expelled from Heaven, and he knows how terrible rejection feels; hence, he will use it as a powerful tool to prevent each one of us from enjoying and worshipping God.

Many of us have been rejected in big or small ways, and in some form by our loved ones who were supposed to care for us. It could have happened because they died, or perhaps you were rejected, like me, because you were born the "wrong" gender. You might have been rejected at school, in the work-place, or even in church ministry where you felt left out in relationships or friendships. But God has not rejected us, and He will never reject us. He loved us so much that He sent His one and only Son, Jesus Christ, to die for our sins. The Lord says even if a mother forgets the baby at her breast and has no compassion on the child she has borne, God will not forget you and me (see Isa. 49:14-15)!

## God Brings a Wonderful Change

So, while growing up, I understood that I did not come from a "normal," happy family; but as I grew older, I eventually began to understand that God had a purpose for all that I had experienced in life. His sovereign will and power had guided and protected me all my life, and His mercies continued to be from everlasting to everlasting. Many other people might not ever face all that I have experienced, but at the same time, I know that there are many others who have suffered through similar experiences and can identify with my story. Perhaps you grew up in a so-called normal, happy family, but one with a non-Christian background, or perhaps one member of your family is schizophrenic, or maybe you were rejected at birth because you were born a girl. Still, there are many others who have gone through even worse and unimaginable pain and agony that cannot be described. If any part of my story speaks to you and your suffering—you see no way out and you have no hope—I urge you to read on.

I beg you to receive the only Person who can come and change your life, who can help you to overcome, who can give you love, life, and make all your dreams come true. His name is Jesus Christ. I urge you to go on an adventure with me. If He can change my life, He can change yours. If He can make a difference in my life and in the life of many other people whom I know, He can make a difference in your life too. It may not be an instantaneous change, but gradually, over time, the change will come. It will happen. He will bring transformation to your life, to your family, and to all that is yours, just as He did mine.

I pray that by the end of this book, you will come face-to-face with a Savior who loves you and that you will embrace His love. He might not come in the way you expect Him to come; there might not be lightning, thunder, or an audible voice. In fact, your life might continue to appear normal and things will seem to go on as usual; but when He turns up, your life will definitely change. God's miracles often occur in the normalcy of life, even while you might not realize or understand it.

As I have walked through the years as a Christian, oftentimes I had no idea of how much God had accomplished in my life. I often did not recognize when He stretched His hand to cover the situations I faced. It was only years later, when I looked back on the path I had walked, saw the footprints in the sand, and reflected on what had happened, that I saw His love and grace littered along the pathway of my life. He left His mark. I did not see Jesus appear visibly in front of me, nor did an angel visit me. I did not hear an audible voice of God, nor did I experience any supernatural physical healings. But I trust that even as you read the rest of this book, you will see God's imprint in the many situations of my life and your life as well. Although we might not always recognize Him, God is definitely in the midst of us.

## ENDNOTES

1. Adrian Rogers, *The Greatest Lesson I've Ever Learned: For Men,* by Bill Bright (Orlando, FL: New Life Publication, 2000).

2. Derek Prince, *Blessing or Curse: You Can Choose* (Christchurch, NZ: Derek Prince Ministries, 1990).

## CHAPTER TWO

# Life in the Church

Hunger means that you're dissatisfied with *the way it has been* because it forced you to live without *Him* in His fullness.....I'm talking about a hunger for God's *presence*.[1]

Tommy Tenny

*Being confident of this very thing, that He which hath begun a good work in you will perform it until the day of Jesus Christ* (Philippians 1:6).

## My Christian Beginning

My aunt was the one who took me to her church when I was about ten years old. It was a traditional church. At first, it was food and recreation that drew my interest. Soon, however, I was attracted to this God who loves me, especially because I was from a home where I was not loved by a father or a mother. I often thought, *Can anyone truly love me and accept all that I am, even though I am a girl?* I was touched that "God so loved the world, that He gave His only begotten Son, that whosoever believeth in Him should not perish, but have everlasting life" (John 3:16).

My brother and I accepted Christ into our lives, and I was baptized on my 13th birthday. A few months after my baptism, my father found out about it and was extremely angry, to the point that he threatened to disown me. I was so frightened that I stopped going to church. But God is good, and through a series of events, He led me to a Christian school where there was regular worship, Scripture reading, and prayer. Though I was not attending church, I was never far from God. Then, when I was 16 years old, I made a decision to go back to church, to my Father's arms of love no matter what sacrifice I had to make or how difficult it might become. And I have been in church ever since.

And so, from the time I was baptized on my 13th birthday to my 27th birthday, I led a normal Christian life in a traditional church. I, along with others in this church, believed in the written Word of God, the Bible, and we lived our lives in accordance to it. All the members of the church were law-abiding, God-loving, and God-fearing men and women. We worshipped God, prayed, held evangelistic events to reach out to our neighborhood, attended renewal camps and participated in normal church activities. But for several years, there was no growth in this church, and eventually, many members started to leave to attend other churches. I had a difficult time understanding why this was happening, and I asked myself many questions. *What did we do wrong? Did we not love them with all our hearts and care for their needs? Did we not show enough concern for them and pray for them?* I could not understand why no breakthrough seemed to be on the horizon.

In any case, I chose to remain in this traditional Chinese church for many years, even though some of my best friends and the people I grew up with had left the church to join charismatic churches. And each Sunday, we continued to practice our rituals of declaring the Lord's Prayer, the Apostles' Creed, the Benediction, and the Dismissal Songs. Some of my relatives also attended the same church every Sunday, and church life was uneventful for many years to come.

## My First Missions Trip

Then in the year 1998, I experienced my very first missions trip for approximately 12 days. About nine members of the church, together with my pastor, traveled into the rural villages of China, where the pastor spoke and conducted seminars while the church members were involved in worship, sharing our testimonies, and organizing a camp for the youth in the village.

Although it was a short trip, I was awed by what I saw, and the experience left a deep impression upon me. This country had been a remote place in my mind, but through this trip, I came to see a China that I never knew existed—a country filled with people of simple faith and a land full of miracles.

As we sat with and spoke to the people who came to attend the church camp, I could not help but wonder why it was that I had never seen a miracle in Singapore, but in China, miracles were abundant. Consequently, I started to believe in the existence of miracles in this present time and age. I used to think that miracles described in the Bible, such as walking on water, raising the dead, supernatural healing, and angelic visitations had ceased to exist, or at best, were few and seldom happened. However, the people of China testified of many personal miracles, some of which follow in the next sections.

## The Village

Two people died. Brother Zhang was a Christian, and Brother Hei, a non-Christian. Brother Zhang was going to Heaven, and Brother Hei to hell. Brother Hei got very upset because Brother Zhang had not shared the Gospel of Jesus Christ with him, even though they had been friends for many years; and he pleaded with Brother Zhang to go to Brother Hei's village of about 150 people to tell them about Jesus Christ. Brother Hei then told Brother Zhang each person's name, occupation, family members, and other village information. At this point, Brother Zhang came back to life. He then went to Brother Hei's village and told them about Jesus, but they did not believe him. However, when Brother Zhang, a stranger who had never been to the village before, started to give exact details of all their names, family backgrounds, occupations, and other information, the people believed and became Christians.

## The Doctor

A doctor was very angry that people were attending church for healing. Then an old woman brought her crippled granddaughter to see this doctor. He informed her that if the little girl ever walked again, he would fall on his knees and crawl for every step that she walked. From the moment those words were spoken, the doctor fell on his knees and has been crippled ever since, while the little girl has recovered.

## The Mad Woman

There was a woman who was left to raise her four children after her husband had died. The fortune-teller had previously told her that she brought bad luck to her family and that her husband and children would die because of her. She was so worried that she went crazy. Then, one sister-in-Christ went to share the Gospel with her and continued to do so many times. The woman mistook this sister as a demon, but the sister did not give up. Finally, the woman believed in Jesus. She was healed and regained her sanity.

### The Woman Who Wanted to Sing

A sister did not know how to read words or chords, but she wanted to sing to the Lord. So she prayed that God would enable her to read words. One night, an old man appeared in her dreams and gave her a book with words and chords. Once she opened it, she could sing. From that very day, every time she has opened a songbook, she has been able to read the words and sing the chords perfectly.

### The Dying Little Girl

A little girl was very sick and dying. Her father had taken her to see many doctors, but none could heal her. Now, she was lying on her bed and could not move. Then, one day, she saw a person in white, who put a pill into her mouth. Once she swallowed it, she immediately became well and could stand and walk. I think that the Lord had visited her and healed her.

# Feeling God's Presence

This trip to China opened my eyes to new spiritual insights, including God's love for His people, faith that still exists, and miracles that are still happening in this age. I feel ashamed when I realize that God has blessed me with a life in a peaceful and prosperous country like Singapore, where I have everything I need materially; yet I still often complain and am dissatisfied. So often what we desire is not something we need as compared to what the people possess in the rural parts of China. I live a life of luxury compared to those people. Their homes are old and dilapidated, their roads are not well-maintained and are very dusty, and their only transportation is to walk, whereas in Singapore we have cheap, efficient, and effective public transportation. Yet many people in China continue to prosper spiritually, and the miracles we hear about touch our hearts. The humble people of China love God, and their hearts burn with fire for Him.

We felt God's presence strongly in the churches and in the gatherings we organized for the church-goers. Even though many people we met had little education and were very poor, they still went out to tell people about God, to share their testimonies, and to spread the Gospel to everyone who would listen, no matter how difficult it was. The church where we ministered was first built with RMB 2300 (renminbi yuan—official currency of China ) ($460) in 1990. Within ten short years, the church grew to 1000 people. Every brick was built with their faith. They prayed and the Lord gave. The spirit and faith of the Chinese people are very much alive, definitely more fervent than that found in many areas of Singapore. Even the elderly people (70 years old and above) walked to and from church for five to six hours so that they could give their busfare—RMB 2 ($0.40)—as an offering to God.

## Waiting for the Baptism of the Holy Spirit

Shortly after we returned from the China missions trip, one of my fellow missionary friends, Victor, left our traditional church to join a charismatic church. I was devastated because he had been one of the first people I befriended when I joined the church. Over the years we had been involved in many evangelistic outreaches, serving in the church as youth leaders and participating in the same youth committee for many years. We grew up together in the church and were very good friends, and I could not understand why he had decided to leave our church. Hurt and in shock, I thought that after such an experience as the China missions trip, Victor would love the Lord even more and would never consider such a thing as leaving our church to join another one. I was upset and confused. Little did I know that eventually, he would be the one instrumental in helping me to move from the realm of the natural to the realm of the supernatural.

When I asked Victor why he decided to leave our church, he told me that he could not remain, because he had determined that there must be something more, especially after witnessing the great spiritual hunger in the people we had met in China. He then had to ask himself if he could continue to remain passionless. He wanted to experience the deep intimacy with God that he had seen within the Chinese people. Consequently, he wrote letters to his mentors and to the leaders of the church to explain his decision to leave the church. He then obtained an official letter of release to transfer to another church. In addition, he told me that it had been very difficult to decide to leave the small church where he had grown up, and where everyone knew each other and their families.

Still, I did not understand. My emotions overwhelmed me and all I could understand was that my good friend was going to another church, and soon we would be like strangers to each other. After he left our church, he started to speak in tongues and would often invite me to his church. He would tell me about the Holy Spirit and explain that I needed to be baptized in the Holy Spirit and speak in tongues. This new information was very confusing to me, and when I did visit his church, I was extremely uncomfortable. The worship was strange—singing in tongues and praying in tongues—none of which I understood, much less wanted to be involved in. It was scary and very weird. I simply could not accept it and could not agree with it. I kept thinking, *How can we speak in another language that we do not understand? It is just not possible. How can such a thing happen in this age and time?* I decided not to be bothered by it, and continued to visit his church over the years because I was hungry and my soul was empty.

The teachings at Victor's church were simple, easy to understand, and very powerful, unlike the boring sermons I had often heard. They were also biblical. When I attended my own church, I sometimes had trouble staying awake during the sermons. I would fidget, and my mind would wander. But when I went to Victor's church, I was more likely to be alert and eager to listen to God's Word. Victor continued to invite me to go to his church. He encouraged me to ask for the baptism of the Holy Spirit and speak in tongues whenever the pastors in his church gave an altar call for people to come forward to receive the gifts. Without fail, every time there was an opportunity, I would go forward and ask...but I never received. And this went on for years.

Then one day, one of my sisters, Pei, also accepted Jesus Christ as her personal Lord and Savior. Subsequently, she was baptized and joined a charismatic church. She too would pester me about speaking in tongues and would often pray to God for me to receive the gift of tongues. I had already believed in Jesus Christ as my Lord and Savior and had been baptized with water at an earlier age, but I could not understand what was so wonderful about speaking in tongues. Furthermore, I had several questions. *What is this talk about another baptism? Is it needed? What good is it?* And while I had many questions, I still had no answers. However, I decided that because two of the people I trusted the most were so adamant that speaking in tongues would be good for me, I should do it. They loved me and wanted only the best for me. Besides, I noticed that Victor was growing in his spiritual walk and faith, and I could visibly see that he had something I did not have, although I still was not very sure what that something was.

So I tried again and again and again to seek and ask for the baptism of the Holy Spirit. But it did not happen for many years. Finally, I reached a point where I told myself it was okay not to speak in tongues or be baptized in the Holy Spirit. I had survived without either and determined that I did not need this baptism. But how wrong I was. I had been missing out on part of the privilege of being a child of God—the fellowship of the Holy Spirit. In the Scriptures, Jesus had asked the disciples to wait in Jerusalem until they were endued with the Holy Spirit power from on high. It was so important that the disciples gathered together in the upper room and waited for the coming of the Holy Spirit.

Oh, beloved, if you do not have the baptism of the Holy Spirit and do not speak in tongues, I beseech you not to give up. I beg you to ask the Father to give you His precious Holy Spirit and eagerly await it from God. His promises never fail; He will give. Perhaps I did not have much faith and I continued to doubt, but God still eventually gave. You must believe that God will give to you too, for He gives good gifts to His children. Ask for it, seek for it, and experience it in your life. It is essential to note that water baptism and Holy Spirit baptism are not substitutes for each other; rather, they complement one another. These two experiences are separate and essential to every believer.

It was only later when I was baptized in the Holy Spirit and started to speak in tongues that I received revelation in my spirit concerning many things. I had been a persecutor of the charismatic church in my youth. I did not understand many things, and what I did not understand, along with many others in the traditional churches, I labeled as bad and of the devil. I thought the charismatic churches came and "stole sheep" from the traditional churches. And we were upset with them because we had no idea that there was more to the Christian life than living a good life. We had no power because we had no knowledge of the Holy Spirit. We knew about the three-in-one God. We knew about God the Father, God the Son, and God the Holy Spirit. But we only knew about them in our minds—not in our hearts or in our experience. We knew of God the Father, and we talked about Him. We knew Jesus Christ as the Son of the living God, the one who came as a man to earth to die on the cross for the sins of the world. Christ was the one who was persecuted, crucified, and eventually resurrected from the dead. We also knew of the person of the Holy Spirit. But we had absolutely no communion or fellowship whatsoever with Him. Oh, we thought we knew who the Holy Spirit was; we thought we knew Him and His purpose. But our pride and our dependence on the Word of God relegated the Holy Spirit to a place of nonexistence in the church.

We continued to dispute and argue the move and works of the Holy Spirit. *What kind of language is this speaking in tongues? Who understands it? How can they claim it is of God? Where does the Bible say it is of God? The tongues have ceased as well as all those things that happened in the Book of Acts. They are no longer relevant in this day and age. What is this talk about being slain in the spirit, holy laughter, and new and strange teachings? What basis is there for all these so-called new revelations? The only revelation is the revealed Word of God contained in the Bible.*

Only many years later did I realize that I had been a pharisee. Forgive me, God, for my ignorance and for my pride. I was like the Pharisees and the Jews who had the Word and knowledge of God, but did not and could not recognize Jesus as the Messiah when He came in a form they could not connect with, in a way they could not understand (see John 8:31-40). So, too, I had failed to recognize and understand the move and the works of the Holy Spirit because they were strange and frightening. I was afraid—afraid of the unknown, afraid of what I could not understand. Oh, how foolish I was. I missed out on so much because of the fear that crippled me and the pride that held me aloof. Yet, oh, how merciful is the love of God.

Though we do not understand, He still has so much patience with us. He still draws us, and He continues to give His Holy Spirit to all who seek Him.

### ENDNOTE

1. Tommy Tenny, *The God Chasers* (Shippensburg, PA: Destiny Image Publishers, 1998), 12-13.

## Chapter Three

# Lost at Sea

Put your complete trust in the Almighty, walk by faith, and you will see *miracles* in your life.[1]

Samuel Doctorian

*Fear not: for I have redeemed thee, I have called thee by thy name; thou art Mine. When thou passest through the waters, I will be with thee; and through the rivers, they shall not overflow thee: when thou walkest through the fire, thou shalt not be burned; neither shall the flame kindle upon thee* (Isaiah 43:1b-2).

## Enjoying Single Life

After Victor left our church, I continued to attend church services every Sunday without fail, and also continued to work and earn a normal living. In

Singapore, people are often consumed with work and spend a large part of their time working, often until very late at night. In addition, I was a very active girl and went out on weekends with my friends. I also loved to travel, so I spent a lot of my money seeing the world, whenever and wherever I could.

At one point, I was involved in a relationship, but after some time I ended it. Sometimes it can seem very suffocating in a relationship where you don't seem to belong to yourself but to your partner. However, with my newfound freedom, I could do whatever I wanted, whenever I wanted, and with whomever I wanted. Hence, I decided to enjoy being single. While my married friends had little time for me, I did have a lot of single friends, and there was always someone to go somewhere or do something with. There were times when I was alone and I felt extremely lonely, but I remembered that being in a relationship was not all good.

Whether you have a partner or are single, there are good aspects as well as bad aspects to both circumstances in life. I decided that because it seemed to be God's desire that I remain single, then I would enjoy being single and make the best of that situation. I purposely decided to focus on the positive attributes of being single and do everything a single person could do that a married person is not so easily able to do because of obvious restrictions. When married, you do not belong to yourself; rather, you belong to your spouse and your children. Your time is consumed with their lives. But whether married or single, we should enjoy our life, for better or for worse. As for me, I lived a carefree life and enjoyed it thoroughly.

## My Romance With Diving

Then in the year 2002, I found a new love—diving. It was such an exciting and fun sport, and I fell in love with it immediately.

But learning to dive was not all that easy. I did not attend a commercial school, such as Padi or Naui; but through a connection with a friend, I learned about the British Sub-Aqua Club (BSAC). Subsequently, I signed up for a diving course.

The training lasted two months, and I attended weekly theory lessons during which the instructors shared with the students the dangers of diving and the importance of taking safety precautions. Personally, I felt this was an overreaction on the instructors' part. I thought diving was as safe as driving or flying an airplane. Sure, there were risks involved, but if we took care to plan the dive and then follow through by diving the plan, we would be all right. *Besides*, I thought, *how many people die during a dive anyway? There are more people killed annually while driving a car or flying in a plane than while diving.*

And so, we continued with our lessons, some of which were really difficult. While many people go to a beautiful island and take a three-day course to become a certified diver, this was not what we experienced at BSAC. Our school was very strict. Our lessons were held in Singapore waters, which were dirty and muddy, and where we were unable to see marine life, coral, or fish. The weekly diving trips out to the seas were not pleasant and were actually terrifying to new and young divers like myself. Yet we did learn many lessons and our confidence in diving continued to build.

During one of our lessons on a particularly rainy day, we went out to an area in the Singapore waters where land reclamation was in progress. Because it was raining, the waters were blackish and sinister, and we had barely submerged five meters when to our horror, someone seemed to have switched off the light completely, and we found ourselves in total darkness. Even when I stretched out my hand, I could not see my fingers in front of me.

We had no torchlights, having not yet learned night diving. So, in panic, my friends and I surfaced from under the water and informed the instructors of the pitch darkness under the sea and of the impossibility to continue to dive. It was our desire to go back on board the boat and head for shore. But to our horror, our instructors informed us that we would not be getting on the boat. Instead, we would be going back down into the waters again, and this time, he wanted us to go right down to the very bottom of the seabed and stay there until he signaled us to come back up.

We thought our instructors had gone crazy, because surely they did not know what they were doing or asking us to do. It had been so dark at five meters; how terrible would it be to go right to the very bottom of the seabed and stay there?! As divers, we certainly wouldn't be able to see each other to encourage or comfort each other down there.

However, our instructors informed us that we had not heard incorrectly and that we were to go down. In fact, they *insisted* that we go down, explaining that this was a once-in-a-lifetime experience. They stated that while we would probably enjoy the most beautiful seas and the most spectacular scenery in the world during our dives in the future, and carry torches during night diving trips, now was the time to learn how not to panic and how to remain calm if we ever faced a dangerous or difficult situation. The instructors informed us that this experience would be the best training ground—that this pitch-black darkness would be the worst enemy we would face underwater.

As students, there was nothing we could do but to obey our instructors. And so, unwillingly, one by one, we went back down under the water, clinging to the rope where the anchor was thrown into the seabed. It was my lifeline, and I refused to let go. My safety, even my life, depended on that rope. When I could not see in the darkness, the rope gave me a peace that transcended all understanding.

This experience reminds me of our Christian walk. There might be times when we walk through deep and terrible darkness, where we can't even see our hand in front of us. Engulfed in pitch darkness, scared and terrified, we want to scream out, but we can't. For if we try to scream through the breathing apparatus, it will mean our death. We must silently face this darkness alone. Our friends might be around us, but we can't see them or derive comfort by looking at their faces for strength. We can only feel them. We have to walk on...alone.

But we do have something—we have the "Rope" to cling to—we have God. Even though we cannot see the Rope, the Rope is there. He is stable, and He will support us.

Trust God in the dark, even when you cannot see Him. Know that the Word is true, that God is beside you always and that He will walk with you every step of the way, even when He doesn't seem to be around and you cannot see His hand. Like the rope, He is still there, stable and dependable.

I went down to the bottom of the seabed and came back up. I survived this ordeal, and I never in my wildest imagination expected that this experience would save my life in the future. Yet because I had gone through this frightening situation and was taught a valuable lesson, I was able to remain calm and collected during one of the most critical and terrifying moments of my diving life.

## Shipwrecked Vivat

Not long after I was certified as an advanced diver, I went on my very first live-on-board diving trip in August 2003. It was a five-day trip, starting at night and returning to Singapore in the wee hours of the morning, effectively giving us three full days of nonstop diving action.

In great anticipation, the 12 of us boarded the *Empress* and set off. I was really excited. Our boat was often right in the middle of the vast ocean with nothing in sight, even when we turned 360 degrees. We dived day and night, and I saw many beautiful life forms under the sea. I could not help but marvel at the wonderful works of God that were beyond description. I had entered a different and silent world, but a world filled with colors and sights unimaginable.

It was the third day of the diving trip, and I had completed nine dives already. I remember the incident very clearly, as though it happened just yesterday. I was extremely tired, but my spirits were up, and I was relishing and enjoying every moment. I was not sure whether I could continue diving because I was exhausted, but when I heard that we would be diving on a shipwreck, I could not resist. How exciting!

Our experienced captain had escorted divers to the Asian waters for diving excursions for more than 20 years. He had previously found hundreds of shipwrecks and had been instrumental in giving the exact location and the GPS (global positioning system) coordinates so that these wrecks could be incorporated in maps for others to use. I felt very safe knowing that he had years of experience under his belt.

He briefed us about the *Vivat*, which sunk in 1917, almost 100 years ago. It was 60 meters in length, and from our boat, the *Empress*, to the bottom of the shipwreck, the maximum depth was 125 feet, which is about 39 meters. He drew a picture of the *Vivat* and explained to us that he would tie a rope from the *Empress* to the *Vivat* and that we could follow the rope down to the bridge, which was about 32 meters deep. He explained that the *Empress* would be above the left-hand corner of the *Vivat* and that a huge net was on the right-hand corner of the sunken ship. He cautioned us to be careful and not go near the net because it could entangle us.

So, in eager anticipation, I made ready to jump into the water. I was slated to go in with one male diver and three other female divers. But because both the male diver and I were ready first, we decided to go ahead without the others. We went underwater and hovered around the bridge while we waited for the rest to descend and join us. We waited for awhile, but the other divers still had not come down. Under the water, the current was strong, and the visibility was bad. It was very cloudy, and I could see only those things that were within an arm's length. That was the beginning of trouble.

My diving partner then signaled to me to let go of the rope and follow him. With the others nowhere in sight, I obeyed his instructions, and we began to explore the *Vivat*. Then he put his thumb up and without waiting for me, he started to ascend. At that point he was experiencing nitrogen narcosis, of which I was not aware. I stood at the bridge staring up at his departing body, and then I made the most taboo mistake in a diver's safety procedures. At any point in time, diving buddies should always be together. Should anything happen and the buddies become separated, a diver needs to ascend immediately. However, I stayed on the bridge alone, still waiting for the others to come down and join me. According to my calculations, I could stay underwater at that depth for about 20 minutes. Any longer would pose a threat to my body.

## *Attempting to Return*

I waited for some time, but the other female divers never showed up. I knew then that I had to begin my ascent. So I looked and searched for the rope that would lead me to safety. But to my horror, there were hundreds of ropes lying on the bridge, and I could not distinguish which one led to the *Empress*. I then decided to take the biggest rope I could find.

Midway up, I came to a place where I saw a huge net with a multitude of fish swimming around, and I immediately knew that I had taken the wrong rope. According to the map that the captain had drawn before we went to explore the shipwreck, I was now on the opposite end of the *Vivat*, away from the *Empress*. As I stopped at the net, I became a bit panicky and unsure of what to do. Then I prayed to God in my heart to help me. I didn't know how to get myself out of this fix, and it was scary to be alone. Then suddenly, an indescribable feeling of peace and calm settled over me, and I knew I would be all right. I cannot quite explain it, but I was sure that I would be safe and that God would bring me through this situation.

At that moment, I had to make an important decision. *Should I go back down and search for the right rope that leads to the **Empress**, or should I continue my ascent?* According to diving safety rules, I could not go back down. Once you dive deep and begin ascending, going back down poses a danger to your life because of the change in air pressure. Hence, I had only one choice—to continue my ascent. This was also dangerous, because if I were to get myself entangled amongst the nets, I had no knife or scissors with me to free myself. But God saved my life, and I successfully ascended without getting caught in the huge net. I was pretty calm at this point, and I could hear the sound of the *Empress's* motor, so I knew that I was near the boat.

Meanwhile, the other divers had returned to the *Empress*, and my partner, suffering from nitrogen narcosis, was being questioned by the rest as to what had happened to me. Another friend had also experienced nitrogen narcosis and started to behave strangely while underwater. However, her boyfriend and another diver, one on each side of her, brought her back from the *Vivat* to the *Empress*. They then did a head count and discovered that I was missing. The group of girls who were supposed to join me had gone down, but because visibility was bad upon reaching the bridge, they had immediately decided to return to the *Empress*.

Then the captain and another very experienced diver went underwater to the *Vivat* in search of me. They also could not find me and surfaced again. When they discovered that I was still not back, at the risk of their own lives, they went back down again to search for me and returned only when their tanks were empty of oxygen. At this point, the people in the boat started to panic while looking through their binoculars and scouring the seas for a sight of me.

Meanwhile, I was trying to remember all the safety procedures that my instructors had tirelessly drummed into our heads during the two months of training at BSAC. This intense training in the dirty waters of Singapore would turn out to be a lifesaver. I had been through a frightening scenario during training; hence, this experience, although scary, was less terrifying then being in a place where I could not even see my hands. At least I could see myself and my surroundings.

I reached my decompression stop at nine meters where I needed to do a one-minute decompression followed by a three-minute decompression at six meters. Then to my horror, I realized that I forgot to wear my watch. I had made yet another diver's mistake. Without my watch, how was I to perform my decompression safety stop? With no other choice, I began the age-old way of counting seconds—"one thousand...two thousand...three thousand...four thousand...." I went on. As I proceeded through my decompression stop, I realized that another problem was at hand—I was drifting away from the *Empress*.

## "Will I Ever Be Rescued?"

The sound of the *Empress's* motor had been loud and clear when I was at the nets, but now as I began my decompression, the sound of the motor started to grow more faint until I could not hear it any longer. I was being swept away by the strong current, and I was trying to decide what to do. Should I immediately stop my safety procedures and surface, or should I continue with my safety stop? By the grace of God, I decided that I needed to do what was right rather than endanger my body and health by surfacing immediately. I had heard stories of people who had surfaced without performing the proper procedures and suffered damage to their health as a consequence. In addition, my instructors had repeatedly reminded us of the importance of completing our safety stops.

So, after completing all the necessary decompression stops, I finally surfaced from underwater, and I was relieved to see the clear blue sky. But my relief was short-lived. When I looked in front of me, I did not see the *Empress*...just the horizon.There was nothing in sight—no boat, no island, nothing—just the vast and limitless ocean. In my head, I imagined the worst. The newspaper headlines read, "Girl Lost at Sea," "Diver Found Dead at Sea." I would be famous overnight, but I was not sure that was the way I wanted to become famous. Once again, I began to pray in my heart. The ocean waves were huge, and my body was exhausted. I prayed to God that when I turned my head, I would see the boat behind me.... Thank God for His mercy and grace, because when I turned around, I saw a tiny dot...and it was the *Empress.*

I was right; the current had been so strong that it had swept me far away. I had no other choice but to fin my way back. Even though my energy was totally depleted, I finned with all the might I had left. But after about 20 minutes, I realized I was not making any progress and I stopped. I had not seemed to have moved any nearer to my destination, and I wondered if the people on the boat could see me. The *Empress* was still so far away, and I began to lose hope.

Then all of a sudden, I heard a sound—it was the sound of a motor. I turned and looked over my shoulders and I saw the captain coming to my rescue in his dingy. I was overwhelmed with relief and gladness, and within a short time, I was back at the *Empress.* They had seen my pink, luminous fins with their binoculars! Those pink fins saved my life!

It's the same in our Christian walk. No matter how hard we try by our own strength, we cannot overcome the difficulties, the sins, or the problems that we face. We can try, we can fight, but we will still end up in the same place and find that we have not moved at all. Our strength is useless, and we are weak. We need a strength that is greater than ourselves. We need God to come in His power and might to rescue us. He will fight through the strong waters and the dangers, the schemes of the enemy, and come to rescue us so that we can be with

Him in His heavenly home. He is our help and deliverer; there is no other. Jesus Christ is the dingy that has come and rescued us from our sins, difficulties, and problems. He died on the cross and exchanged His life for ours. He was punished so that we might be forgiven, wounded so that we might be healed.

That day, I learned that diving can be a dangerous sport and that I need to be careful at every step in order to preserve my life. I made many mistakes during that particular diving trip, and many dangerous events happened. I could have lost my life during any point in time. But thank God for His protection and that I am alive today to tell this tale. It was a scary experience—alone on a shipwreck, lost at sea, not knowing what to expect, and a narrow escape from the clutches of death. Yet strangely enough, I felt a supernatural peace and calm throughout the ordeal, and I was able to perform all the right techniques and safety procedures. I was completely protected by God, and throughout the experience, I was assured that I would see the daylight once again. Despite the dangers, I knew in my heart that I would be safe and sound. God was with me all the way, and He carried me through.

### ENDNOTE

1. Samuel Doctorian, *My Daily Strength* (Jakarta, ID: Immanuel Publishing House), 141.

CHAPTER FOUR

# Can This Be Tongues of the Devil?

*Revelation* takes us only halfway there; *experience* leads us all the way.[1]

Bill Johnson

*For he that speaketh in an unknown tongue speaketh not unto men, but unto God: for no man understandeth him; howbeit in the spirit he speaketh mysteries* (1 Corinthians 14:2).

## A Strange and Disturbing Experience

My first encounter with strange happenings in the churches of Singapore occurred when I was about 15 years of age in the 1980s. Although I had come from a traditional church, which did not move in the power of the Holy Spirit nor speak in tongues, I had friends who spoke in tongues. In my secondary school, there were friends who attended charismatic churches and who would speak to me about tongues. I had many questions for them, but no one could give me a satisfactory answer or an answer that I could understand. In fact, I considered the responses vague and rather evasive.

Then one day, one of them invited me to attend a charismatic gathering to see firsthand what it was all about. (I suspect that they were frustrated with my questions and decided to take me to a service, hoping I would see and understand, and subsequently stop asking them questions they could not answer.)

With great anticipation, I went. And although it has been more than a decade since I went to that gathering and I cannot remember the name of the church, the friend who took me, or the address of the church, I can remember some of the things that happened during that visit. I was terrified and shocked by all kinds of strange things happening around me, and I told myself I would never go to these so-called charismatic meetings again. And for almost 15 years thereafter, I kept that promise, until God Himself, through a series of events, brought me face-to-face with the charismatics once again.

This time was the beginning of the charismatic movement in Singapore, where many are still learning to move by the Holy Spirit and casting out demons. This was also the period where many of the charismatic churches were founded. However, the day that I first visited the charismatic church, the only thing I could remember was that it was very chaotic. There were people running all around the room, others were screaming, others were laughing, and others were lying on the floor. (And these things were not my image of what a church should look like. At that time, I remember thinking that God is a God of order and not chaos, and a church should not be chaotic. Hence, this was a very disturbing scene to my eyes.)

This particular service was my very first encounter with the charismatic, and I came out of it very shaken and in great fear. At that time, I did not realize that God had other plans for me or that I would move from one extreme of the spectrum (Bible believing, no-nonsense traditional church) to the other spectrum (living by the Holy Spirit and learning to walk with Him in a charismatic church). But in the end, it was God's good and perfect plan.

## A Desire Is Birthed and Increases

I had no deep knowledge of who the Holy Spirit was, let alone how to move by the power of the Holy Spirit; however, I studied and clung to the Bible, the Word of God. Then when I did move into the realm of the Holy Spirit, I had both the Word of God and the baptism of the Holy Spirit. Each personal experience and revelation must be in line with the revealed Word of God. We must have both the Word of God and the baptism of the Holy Spirit. For without the Holy Spirit, the power of the Word is greatly diminished; and without the Word, the Holy Spirit can move but not at full potential and power. Both must move in tandem with each other. One without the other is like someone who has lost one of his hands or eyes or legs. We can still function without one of those body parts, but we can never function to the fullest potential as when we are complete and are operating with our entire set of body parts.

For many years I stayed away from the charismatic movement and such experiences as the Toronto blessings and holy laughter. In fact, I avoided all things related to the charismatic realm like a plague, until 1998 when I returned from the missions trip to China. As I mentioned before, at that time, one of my good friends, Victor, left our traditional church to join a charismatic church. Victor then started to share with me about many things with regard to the baptism of the Holy Spirit, speaking in tongues, the *rhema* word of God he had received, the *logos* Word of God, the season he was in, and the things he was learning. Although I tried to understand what he was saying, I could not fully comprehend it. It seemed to hit my brain but would then slip out, never being received in my inmost being and hence never fully understood.

All along I had hoped that going to a charismatic church for Victor would be just a phase and that one day he would return to our traditional church. We all would look back and laugh about one of those fads that young people often get caught up in. But slowly, over time, I came to realize that he would never return because he had found something better. I saw that Victor was happy, much happier than when he was with us. Furthermore, spiritually, he was growing tremendously, whereas I was stagnant, not learning and not growing. Sure, I was attending church regularly on Sundays and listening to sermons and reading God's Word and Christian literature, but I knew I had not grown for years. Yet every time I saw Victor and heard his stories, I would ask myself many questions and consider that perhaps Victor was right. Perhaps there was something about this Holy Spirit and baptism that he kept telling me about that I needed to experience for myself. For sure, there was something missing, but I didn't know what it was.

Eventually, the desire to be baptized in the Holy Spirit and to speak in tongues was birthed in me, and this desire increased when my sister became a Christian and went to a charismatic church. Both my sister and Victor kept encouraging me as I continued to ask and pray for the baptism of the Holy Spirit. As I mentioned before, I even went to the front of the room during services so that the pastor could pray for me to receive it. This went on for many years, and still nothing happened. I never received the so-called baptism of the Holy Spirit or was able to speak in tongues. Why? I do not know. But it did not bother me. I figured God probably did not want to give it to me and that it was probably useless anyway. And so I left it at that. I gave up until unexpectedly God decided to give it to me.

## *An Encounter With God*

I still remember the day when I was baptized in the Holy Spirit and started to speak in tongues. It was during an "Encounter With God" weekend camp with my sister's church. For many years, while I was in a traditional church and my sister was in a charismatic church, she had invited me to attend this "Encounter With God" camp held regularly in the hotels of Singapore—a weekend where you go to encounter and spend time with God. It usually started on a Friday evening and ended on a Sunday evening. For many years, I refused to attend, and then in September 2003, about two weeks before I left Singapore to go to London, I just had a desire to attend this camp. And so, when my sister once again invited me to go, I accepted. Some of the topics that were covered included the joy of forgiveness, redemption, family, faith to heal the soul, and baptism of the Holy Spirit.

I don't remember much of what happened during the camp or what I learned; I can only remember the moment when I was baptized in the Holy Spirit and started to speak in tongues. This experience shocked me because it was not the reason I had decided to go, and furthermore, I had reached a stage where I told myself that it was all right to live without speaking in tongues.

It happened on the last day of the camp while I was attending a teaching session on the baptism of the Holy Spirit. After the class, those who had not received the baptism were prayed for. I remember being surrounded by many people who prayed for me to receive the gift of the Holy Spirit. Then they asked me to open my mouth and speak. I was about to open my mouth to tell them that it would fail like every other time when I prayed for speaking in tongues, but what came out of my mouth was not the words that I wanted to say. Instead, a long string of a "foreign language" that I did not understand and could not understand burst forth. In shock, I quickly closed my mouth and stopped. Everybody around me was so happy and confidently said, "Yes, you have definitely received the gift of the Holy Spirit. You were speaking in tongues just now!" Everyone was praising the Lord and was overjoyed for me. This was the beginning of my journey.

## Doubts and Fears

After that day, however, my mind was in a whirl, and I was afraid. I had many doubts, fears, and questions. *What if this tongues that I spoke is not of God but is of the devil? How do I know for sure that this was from God? Why is it that I could not understand a single word that came out of my mouth?* Maybe it was a fluke and I just happened to speak some gibberish that everyone thought was speaking in tongues.

It was an unknown arena to my traditional church mentality and background. I could not tell or ask anyone in my traditional church about what had happened because no one in that church spoke in tongues. In fact, many people in that church were *opposed* to speaking in tongues and often verbally spoke against it. My Christian friends whom I had known for the past 16 years of my Christian walk could not help me or give me a greater understanding of what was happening. Only Victor and my sister could do that. Of course, there was another problem. In two weeks, I was leaving Singapore to go to London and would probably not return for two years. It was a challenge and a journey that I felt I had to take, and there was no turning back. I could only trust God that He would know what was best for me.

I was told that when you start to speak in tongues, it is talking to God spirit to spirit, and just like a baby who starts talking with sounds, short words, and phrases, I would likewise practice speaking in tongues. As it became more and more familiar, it would start sounding more like a language. But the problem was, I was afraid to try to start to speak in tongues again, simply because it was not a language my intellect could comprehend or understand. I had graduated from the local university in Singapore and had majored in finance. I was a very systematic and logical person, whereas everything about this baptism in the Holy Spirit and speaking in tongues was illogical and incomprehensible to me. *Should I continue practicing it? Should I continue speaking in tongues?* I was in a great dilemma, and I knew that it would probably become worse when I arrived in London alone where I wouldn't know anyone except one friend who was not a Christian.

But then again, while I was involved with all the preparations of getting ready to live in a foreign country for the first time in my life, speaking in tongues became the last thing on my mind. I just left it at that and occasionally spoke in tongues when no one was around and I was alone in my room. At other times, when I was fearful and questioned whether speaking in tongues was of God or the devil, I would then simply stop speaking in tongues. And it all eventually came to an end three months after I arrived in London. My journey took an unexpected turn, and I embarked on another adventure—a Discipleship Training School (DTS) through Youth With a Mission (YWAM) in the beautiful country of Scotland.

## *Gaining Knowledge and Understanding*

During a period of less than one year after I started to speak in tongues, I began to notice something. I had started to listen to other people as they spoke in tongues and to myself as I spoke in tongues. I noticed that my spirit seemed to rise and move within me when I spoke in tongues, and I sensed the presence of God very deeply and strongly. I also noticed that some people around me were speaking in the same tongues as I was, whereas others were speaking in different tongues from me; and I recognized that different tongues were being spoken by different people. It is similar to hearing someone speak Japanese and another person speak Malay; although I don't speak either language and cannot understand either one, I can recognize that two different and distinct languages are being spoken. Over time, as I practiced speaking in tongues more often, I was no longer fearful; on the contrary, there was a peace in my spirit that I knew was from God.

And of course, as I started to study and read more about this phenomenon of speaking in tongues, I began to understand more. From the book entitled *On the Holy Spirit*[2] by Smith Wigglesworth, I learned that when I received the Holy Spirit, I received the Spirit of truth. It was the Holy Spirit that enabled me to speak in tongues, and because He is the Spirit of truth, speaking in tongues had to be of God (see John 14:16-17). In fact, when you receive the Holy Spirit, you receive the Spirit who gives revelation (see John 14:26). I know for a fact that my understanding of the Bible and what it says has increased tremendously since the time I was baptized in the Holy Spirit, and I know that this understanding and revelation is from the Holy Spirit. I cannot imagine a life without His companionship and fellowship. When you receive the Holy Spirit, you receive the Spirit who takes the words of Jesus and makes them life to you (see John 16:15).

I personally am to blame for not having been filled with the Holy Spirit and not having received the gift of tongues sooner. It is no wonder that it was many years before God finally had mercy on me and gave me the promise that Jesus gave to all His disciples after He died and rose again. At that time, Jesus instructed the disciples to wait in Jerusalem for the gift that the Father promised (see Acts 1:4-5). The Bible says that you do not have because you do not ask (see James 4:2). Many believers of Jesus Christ do not get baptized in the Holy Spirit and do not move in the gifts of the Holy Spirit, including but not limited to speaking in tongues, because many have failed to ask God the Father for the gift of God the Holy Spirit, which God the Son Jesus Christ promised. Others, like me, might ask for many years for the gifts, but never receive because of unbelief. Yet we need to believe God and what He says, because He is able to do immeasurably more than we can ask or hope for or imagine.

Of course, another common barrier is *doubting* that God can fill *us* with the Holy Spirit, even while we acknowledge that He has done so for others. We compare ourselves to others and think we are not spiritual enough, not holy enough, or not good enough; and we come to the conclusion that God will not give to us. We doubt the Father, the goodness of God, and the love of God. And of course, the most gripping of all barriers that comes before, during, and after the baptism of the Holy Spirit and speaking in tongues is *fear*. There is in each of us a fear of the unfamiliar, fear of the supernatural, fear of the incomprehensible and unexplainable, because our logical and intellectual minds need to see and hear things that we can touch or recognize, none of which happens in the realm of the spirit.

Many things that happen are difficult, if not impossible, to explain. How do you describe to people or allow them to see what you experience in the spirit realm? I hear of people meeting angels or seeing Jesus; I find that awesome and intriguing, yet I know that no matter how much people try to explain or describe their experience to me, I will never be able to fully understand and comprehend it until I myself walk through it. And so it is with describing the gift of speaking in tongues and other gifts of the Holy Spirit. Communication cannot just touch the human mind; it must touch the human spirit, because God has said in His Word that true worshippers must worship God in spirit and in truth (see John 4:24). How can I truly understand what Scripture says if I do not have a living and walking comprehension of what "spirit" itself means? If I do not understand that man is made up of three parts—spirit, soul, and body (see 1 Thess. 5:23) and do not know who the Holy Spirit really is, then how can I communicate with the Holy Spirit?

It was only when I myself spoke in tongues that I began to understand why none of my friends could give me an answer that satisfied me when I asked them about speaking in tongues. They tried to explain to me in the spirit, but I was listening and trying to understand in my soul (my mind and intellect). When most people get baptized in the Holy Spirit and speak in tongues, they just leave it at that. Many times, their family and friends in church around them have spoken in tongues for many years. It was never threatening and was considered perfectly normal. Most people don't question the authenticity of speaking in tongues in a charismatic church; they just speak it. Even though I had many questions before I spoke in tongues, once I started to speak in tongues, all the questions became redundant or unimportant. There was no longer a need to know all the answers. I just spoke in tongues, and as I practiced doing it, it slowly became a lifestyle and a form of communication. The fears, doubts, and questions were forgotten over a period of time.

It can be compared to learning how to drive a car. When you don't know how to drive a car, you observe other people driving and you might ask many questions, attempting to understand not only how to drive but how all parts of the car operate. But when you eventually learn and have mastered the art of driving the car, it is no longer important to know how the car works; you simply drive the car. You do not need to know everything about the car in order to drive the car. Hence, in the same way, you do not need to know everything about the Holy Spirit or speaking in tongues to be able to speak in tongues or move in the gifts of the Holy Spirit. While some basic understanding is required, the rest will be built up as you grow in maturity and you learn along the way. However, just as you cannot drive the car unless you learn about the basics, such as how to operate the ignition, acceleration, brakes, and the clutch, so you cannot speak in tongues or move in the power of the Holy Spirit unless you also understand the basics. (Please see Appendix 1—Basics About the Holy Spirit, for a better understanding of who the Holy Spirit is.)

## ENDNOTES

1. Bill Johnson, *The Supernatural Power of a Transformed Mind* (Shippensburg, PA: Destiny Image Publishers, 2006).

2. Smith Wigglesworth, *On the Holy Spirit* (New Kensington, PA: Whitaker House, 1998).

CHAPTER FIVE

# Leaving My Country and My Home

We long for *adventure*, to be caught up in something larger than ourselves, a drama of heroic proportions. It's part of our design.[1]

Brent Curtis and John Eldredge

*By faith Abraham, when he was called to go out into a place which he should after receive for an inheritance, obeyed; and he went out, not knowing whither he went* (Hebrews 11:8).

## There Must Be Something More

I first thought seriously about going to London in September 2002. A friend of mine had decided to go to London to work for two years, and she asked me if

I would consider going as well. From that day until I eventually built up the courage to go to London, God gave me three opportunities.

I had been hesitant to leave Singapore. It had been a safe and secure environment for so many years, and it seemed a foolish thing to go to London for two years and then come back to Singapore and try to catch up with the rat race. My siblings and I had been brought up, living in a "straight path," where children are expected to get a good education, complete a degree at a university, and go on to work, get married, and have children. And the cycle repeats itself with each new generation. It is the unspoken norm in our society of Singapore. Occasionally, there are people who go off the beaten track, but it is not common.

At that time, although I had been a Christian for many years and seldom failed to attend a single service, I still felt an emptiness in my heart that I could not put my finger on. I was lacking something, but I had no idea what it was. I had heard that there is a space in our heart that only Jesus Christ can fill. Nothing else (not work, family, or other relationships) can fill that void. Hence, having been a Christian for many years, I thought that the void should have already been filled. So why was there this emptiness and hunger in my heart? Why did I feel that something was missing from my life?

For one year before I left Singapore to go to London, I attended three to four services a week at different churches, including my own church. I was hungry and desperate and feeling restless. So much had recently happened—the September 11, 2001 bombing of the Twin Towers in New York City, the December 2002 Bali bomb, and the February-to-May 2003 SARS outbreak in Singapore and various Asian countries. The world had changed since 9-11, and it was no longer a world we could recognize. Terrorism had arrived on the scene, and life was no longer safe, even in peaceful Singapore. For the first time in my life as a Singaporean, I saw soldiers everywhere—at the airports, train stations, and along the streets.

I was bored with the life and the job I had. Sure, I had money and could travel all around the world, eat in fancy restaurants, and do most anything I wanted to do; but I could not get rid of the sickening feeling inside of me—that there must be something more to life than this. Working had its usual stress, relationship issues, feelings of inadequacy, being reprimanded for things I hadn't done, falsely accused by others, and being looked down on by others. It was all part and parcel of "normal life," but I couldn't help but question this life. If I continued to stay and work in Singapore, then this normal routine life would continue, probably until the day I died and met with the Lord.

On the other hand, change would be good, but it would also be scary. An unknown future overseas seemed very shaky. Yet I remembered someone once said that *faith* was spelled r-i-s-k. So, I pondered for about one year on whether or not I should go to London. I had been to London once before in 1997, after I graduated from university; and although it was a gloomy place, with dark and depressing weather and old buildings, it did have its charms.

I continued to struggle with my decision whether to go or not. Although I was risking a stable, predictable life, it seemed a wonderful idea to go to London to work and at the same time take the opportunity to travel around Europe. Furthermore, two years seemed a very short time, and I already had one friend there. I told myself that if I didn't take the opportunity to go now, I would probably never go, especially if I got married.

Then I would have even more considerations, such as housing loans, car loans, and a husband and children to consider. I was not getting any younger, and I had never lived in a foreign country for longer than one month. I did not want to have any regrets. I didn't want to look back ten years from now and realize I had an opportunity to go on an adventure and live a different lifestyle but was too afraid to even try.

I felt as though there was a voice beckoning and drawing me to London. I had no idea what it was that was calling me to go, but it became more and more intense by the day. It finally reached a point where I felt that I had to go. No matter what happened, good or bad, I had to go to London. But then again, I also continued to consider the financial risks and the sacrifice. My sister and I were the sole breadwinners of the family. There were considerations besides myself before I could make a decision.

## God Says, "Go"

Finally, in September 2003, one night as I was reading my devotions, I felt as though God was speaking to me, as though He knew what I was facing and what I was worried about. He could read my mind and gave me an answer that only He could give. The following passage by John Macbeath taken from *"Streams in the Desert and Springs in the Valley"* devotional convicted me that it was God's will for me to go to London.

After the resurrection, the disciples were bewildered, and the way looked black. But the angel said, "Behold, He goeth *before you* into Galilee." He is always ahead, thinking ahead, preparing ahead. Take this text with you into the future, take it into today's experience: "Let not your heart be troubled, neither let it be afraid.... I go to prepare a place for you." He is out in the world doing it. *He* will be there *before you*. He will bring you to your appointed place and you will find your *appointed resources*. You will discover *His insight, His oversight and His foresight*. You may not always see Him, but you can walk by faith in the dark if you know that He sees you, and you can sing as you journey, even through the night.[2]

After I read the above passage, I wrote in my journal, "Wow! God knows my fears and provided His assurance in anticipation of it. I must go to London and fulfill His destiny for me." The very next day, I wrote my resignation letter and prepared to go overseas.

## Considering a Short Detour

But before I left Singapore to go to London, I had to do something that I had wanted to do since 2001—something that one of my good friends, Kit, told me that she did—a Discipleship Training School (DTS) through Youth With a Mission (YWAM) in Singapore. This training was a six-month course—three months learning about various aspects of God and three months of missions work. She had told me much about this school, and it sounded marvelous. At that time, I thought the school was located only in Singapore, and Kit informed me that they taught subjects, including "How to Hear the Voice of God," "Spiritual Warfare," "Holy Spirit," "Father, Heart of God," and many other interesting topics that were never taught or even spoken about in my traditional church. Kit told me amazing stories of her foreign schoolmates who had no money to go on outreaches yet who were miraculously provided for by God. She told me stories of how God spoke and how they would listen and ask God which nation they should go to. It all sounded so amazing to me, and I wanted so much to go.

But when I first spoke to my sister in 2001 about my desires, she became extremely angry with me, insisting that I was a selfish person to want to do something like this and leave her with the financial burden of the family. Although she was a Christian, she accused me of all kinds of horrible things. Consequently, I became upset and was convinced that it was not right for me to take six months off work, spending thousands of dollars to attend a DTS, while not earning an income for my family. Although I wanted to go to DTS to learn more about God and acquire a deeper understanding and walk with Him, it seemed impossible. My sister had agreed that I should go to London to work as long as I could send money home, but to attend DTS was a different matter. Eventually, however, she agreed for me to apply at the Discipleship Training School in Singapore because she knew how much I wanted to go.

And so, I applied to attend the DTS in Singapore and told myself that if I was accepted, I would stay in Singapore and not go to London. However, it was not to be. I was not accepted, and so I left for London, never realizing that it was indeed God's will for me to attend a DTS, but just not in Singapore. He had other plans.

## The Path According to God's Will

I left Singapore, my country and my home, and flew to London. The few months living in London was not easy. Although there were plenty of jobs, and the economy did not seem to be as affected by the world events as much as Singapore had been affected, and I went for lots of interview, somehow the doors for jobs remained tightly shut. Consequently, I became anxious and a bit depressed. It was expensive to live in London; the exchange rate at that point was £1 to $3 (Singapore rate). For example, to eat a plate of chicken rice in Singapore cost $2, but to eat one in London cost about £5, which was equal to about $15 in Singapore. It was exorbitant, and it did not even taste as good as the food in Singapore.

Eventually, I was hired for a temporary job while looking for a more suitable one. After a month or so, my sister and I became worried and started to pray more fervently, seeking the Lord. Then one day, my sister told me that she heard the word "mission," and she felt I was supposed to be involved in missionary work in the United Kingdom. At first, I was puzzled. And then it struck me—could it be Youth With a Mission? Could it be that it was God's will for me to attend a Discipleship Training School in London?

And so I started communicating with two YWAM schools in and near London. But in early December 2003, I was informed by both schools that they could not accept me. One of the schools was full and could not accept additional students while the other school did not have a DTS. And so I was thrown into an even greater state of confusion. I cried out to God, asking for answers, but as usual, there was no reply. Silence. Wasn't God supposed to speak? I thought Kit had told me that we could hear God's voice. However, I had been a Christian for so many years but had never heard His voice. Why was it that when I desperately needed Him, needed to hear His voice, that there was no answer? How come my cries and prayers seemed to beat against an impregnable wall? Was God listening? Did He answer prayers? Was He sleeping? I had many questions but no answers.

A few days later, unexpectedly, I received an email from one of the YWAM schools in Scotland, asking if I was interested in applying at the DTS there. Apparently, the London YWAM schools had forwarded my DTS query to other schools in the UK. I had never been to Scotland and had no idea where this school was, but I thought that maybe, just maybe, this was the school where God wanted me to complete my DTS.

Subsequently, I replied to the school administrator, informed her that I was interested, and asked if she would kindly email me the application forms to complete for admission into the DTS in January 2004. She replied that she would send the application form via post mail. This concerned me because I was going to Austria from December 11 to December 15, 2003 for my very first solo travel trip and would not return until midnight, December 15. I explained that the post had to reach me before I left for Austria, and she informed me that my application form had to be returned to Scotland by December 17, 2003. If it did not reach them by that date, I would not be considered for the DTS. It was very important that I adhered to the strict closing deadline as the leaders of the school had to pray about each applicant before they could accept someone. If the application came after the December 17th deadline, they would have to reject the application. It was another round of shocking news to my already weak heart.

On top of all these deadlines that I had to adhere to, provided the application form reached me, I had another problem. London was experiencing a postal strike, on and off, during that period of time, and I heard that some people had not received their mail for a month. There was also another problem—I had to work the whole day on December 16th. Furthermore, I had not been to the local post office in London and didn't have a clue where it was or how long it would take to send a letter from London to Scotland. It seemed that it would take a miracle for me to even send in my application form!

Unfortunately, to my dismay, December 10, 2003 came and went with no sight of the mail carrying my DTS application forms. When I left London to travel to Austria on December 11th, there was still no sight of the application forms. So, I decided to enjoy myself and the sights in Austria. When I returned on December 15, 2003 at midnight, I completed the forms that very night, and the next day during lunchtime, I took my precious application form to a post office some distance away from my workplace and mailed my letter. Praise the Lord, they had an express, one-day delivery service from London to Scotland. (Of course, that was provided that no one went on strike.) I called the YWAM school in Scotland two days later and was informed that they had received all five application forms needed to consider my admittance for DTS. They advised me to go for a medical checkup, part of the requirement for admittance, and they also informed me that I would receive their reply between January 5th and January 9th, 2004, as to whether I had been accepted or not.

### ENDNOTES

1. Brent Curtis and John Eldredge, *The Sacred Romance* (Nashville, TN: Thomas Nelson, 1997).

2. John Macbeath, *Streams in the Desert and Springs in the Valley,* by Mrs. Charles E. Cowman, September 13 issue, (Grand Rapids, MI: Zondervan Publishing House, 1996), 259.

## CHAPTER SIX

# The Darkest Hour Comes Just Before Dawn

Don't stop one *prayer* short of the miracle.

A friend from Norway

*We were pressed out of measure, above strength, insomuch that we despaired even of life: But we had the sentence of death in ourselves, that we should not trust in ourselves, but in God which raiseth the dead* (2 Corinthians 1:8-9).

## A Real Estate Miracle

At this point in time, my sister called me from Singapore and asked me to return to settle the purchase of a flat for our family. My family had been living in the western tip of Singapore for some years, and in

1999, we had decided to sell our flat and purchase another one. However, it was not to be an easy task.

My sisters and I were disturbed by the idolatrous altar that our father had brought home when we moved to Jurong. My eldest sister claimed that she saw faces on the wall in her bedroom, and there were many times when I felt uncomfortable at home and sensed that someone was watching me or entering my room late at night when I was sleeping. But then again, I would think that most of the feelings were figments of my wild imagination. There were also instances when the idol in our home shifted overnight and had to be readjusted almost every other day, along with many other strange happenings at home.

Besides all these strange occurrences, there was the issue that our flat was far away from the city center, which meant longer traveling time to places in Singapore. We often had to change various modes of transportation when going anywhere in Singapore, including bus and train transportation.

So just before I left for London, we decided to find another agent to help us sell our flat. The new agent had helped my brother buy his flat a few months before, and she agreed to help us as well, although she was reluctant because the resale of flats at that time was very slow and the selling prices were low. She warned us that it would take a miracle to sell our flat and advised us not to get our hopes up. She also informed us that she had been trying to sell another flat in the Jurong area for many months, but to no avail, even though that flat was in a better location than our flat and on a much higher floor (ninth floor compared to our third-floor flat). In addition, our flat was blocked on three sides by other flats and was next to a primary school, which could be noisy and disturbing at times. Furthermore, it was inconveniently located and not close to any Mass Rapid Transit (MRT) stations, the main form of transport for Singaporeans. She alerted us that even if the flat could be sold, it would be sold below its market value. We assured her that we were aware of all these facts, and would pray and believe God to help us.

Miraculously, two weeks after I arrived in London, I was informed by my sister that someone knocked on the door of our house, requesting to buy our flat in order to live near their parents. The agent declared that it was a miracle—because not only did we sell it, but we sold it above the market value.

Consequently, we needed to find a new flat within three months. Because I was in London, my sister was the one who needed to search for a suitable flat that would meet all the needs of our family, which was not easy. She visited more than 30 flats and became very frustrated. Nothing met even some of our criteria. So, she demanded that I return to Singapore to settle the buying of a flat. I booked a flight and traveled to Singapore on the last day of 2003 and the first day of 2004.

## *Another Real Estate Miracle*

I could understand the frustration that my sister was facing, trying to find a suitable flat and dealing with all of the family's criteria. We had established a maximum amount that we could spend on a downgrade from a five-room flat to a four-room flat. In addition, we wanted a flat located within Tiong Bahru and Clementi, and within walking distance from the MRT. My mom also wanted the flat to be within walking distance from the market so that it would be convenient for her to go and buy food for preparation on a daily basis. Furthermore, my sister wanted a flat that was fully renovated and in move-in condition because we had no money for renovations.

I remember coming back in January 2004 on a Thursday and starting to pray. I thought I had heard God say that everything would be settled by Tuesday; but I thought that I probably hadn't heard correctly, and it was probably just my imagination. Besides, my sister had already been searching for a suitable flat for three months, but to no avail. Then, on Saturday, I met with the agent to view some flats. After showing me three of the flats that my sister was interested in but which did not fully meet our criteria, she asked me if I was interested in seeing a six-room flat. I told her that a six-room flat was too big for my family, but out of curiosity, I decided to take a look at what a jumbo flat was like.

When I first entered the flat, I immediately marveled that it met all the criteria that our family had set. So I returned with my sister to see the flat on Sunday, and on Monday we took our parents to also see the flat. Later that day, after a series of discussions with the owners on the phone, by God's grace, we bought the flat at a price we could afford. The most amazing fact was that this flat met all that we had asked for and more.

God had taken into account that there were three daughters living with their parents in the same flat, and He gave each of us our own room for privacy. As we had prayed for, the flat was located within Tiong Bahru and Clementi and within walking distance to the MRT. It was also within walking distance to the market. It came fully renovated and in move-in condition. On top of all our criteria, my bedroom had a walk-in wardrobe, which I had wanted for years after I visited my friend's home and saw how lovely her wardrobe was, but had never dared to dream that I could possibly own one.

Each of the bedrooms had air conditioners except for one, which catered exactly to the very needs of our family. My one sister did not enjoy having an air conditioner in her room, as she often woke up in the morning with sinus and cold problems. God's amazing attention to details is remarkable.

## *Waiting for God to Turn Up*

With the purchase of the flat settled, I still had other worries on my mind. I decided that whether I was accepted into the Discipleship Training School in Scotland or not, I would still return to London. If I was accepted, I would go to Scotland; and if I was rejected, I would remain in London. But my heart's desire was to attend DTS. And so, with the little faith I had, I was able to buy an airplane ticket from London to Scotland, while I waited at home for an answer to my application.

In the meantime, since the first day I had arrived in Singapore, I had also been trying to purchase a plane ticket through at least ten different airlines, traveling from Singapore to London; and I discovered that the only available seats were in business and first class, which I could not afford. All other seats were filled until February.

Waiting those one and a half weeks in Singapore was sheer agony—not knowing if I would be accepted into the DTS program. I was very anxious, distressed, confused, and uneasy. The only thing I could do was pray and wait...and that was what I did. In addition, I opened my email box a few times each day, especially on the week that YWAM Scotland promised me I would receive my answer—between the 5th and 9th of January. But each day, I faced another disappointment.

Indeed, I once heard someone say, "The darkest hour comes just before dawn," and I thought this was so true. The most difficult and agonizing time comes just before receiving the answer, before the light, before revelation, before God unfolds His plans and His will. Waiting is not always easy, no matter what we are waiting or hoping for. Perhaps we are waiting for the birth of a child, an increase in salary, a promotion, the right person to marry, God's financial provision, physical healing, or the results of an important exam or election. But no matter what it is that we are waiting for, it is often not easy. Many times, we would rather have an answer, even if it is bad news, rather than be in the mode of waiting. But while waiting can be difficult, it is also often a time to discover if we will give up or if we will persevere and press on and believe in our God to help us.

There is a cycle in the process of waiting. God says something, and I believe in Him. Then circumstances and events happen that seem to be the very opposite of what God has declared. And because I do not see the coming of His promise, I start to doubt, question, and disbelieve what God has said. Then out of the blue and out of God's mercy, the events happen exactly as God has promised they would. It is then that I realize that God has never changed; rather, it was I who was swayed by what I saw with my physical eyes. I should always remain in what God says and believe that it will be so, no matter what happens in the physical realm. Sometimes it takes a period of time—months or even years—before we can see God's promises come to fruition.

## *Overcoming More Obstacles*

Praise the Lord—the long-awaited answer came on January 9, 2004, when I was informed that I had been accepted to the DTS in YWAM Scotland, and school would start in one week's time on January 17. So much had happened in the short one month since I had sent my letter to the school, and now I had one week to get injections and make all the necessary preparations before I could join the school. In addition, there were many problems to overcome—I had to raise funds, obtain a correct visa, and purchase an airline ticket from Singapore to London…all in one week.

I had some savings but needed more finances. Going to the DTS was not something I had planned, and hence, I had not prepared for this extra financial cost, which would be approximately $10,000 just for school fees and an airline ticket to Scotland. I hadn't forgotten what the administrator had told me with regard to finances—"The provision of finances is God's seal of approval." Those were such anointed words, such words of wisdom. And indeed, amazingly, I managed to raise half my school fees within one week. Most of the finances came from unexpected places and unexpected people, one of whom was a director from my previous company whom I had met at an Encounter Weekend Camp in September 2003. (God's timing and His ways are beyond understanding.) After I emailed a note to several people, asking them to consider supporting me financially as well as praying for me, she happened to be the person who gave me almost half the finances that I raised. Indeed, God was bringing me to my appointed place and appointed resources.

Meanwhile, I was on the wrong visa, and YWAM Scotland wanted me to exchange my current visa for another one. But I had only one week in which to change the visa, which seemed impossible to do, even in efficient Singapore. After corresponding with Scotland via email and telephone, with regard to many issues that I needed to settle within one week, the school leaders finally told me they needed to pray and seek God's will, whether I could retain the visa I was holding or change my visa. By God's grace, after much prayer, the leaders allowed me to come to DTS with my current visa; and so, God removed another obstacle in my pathway.

During that week, I also had to be vaccinated against all kinds of possible diseases; and I had to prepare other health-related documents, attempt to get a required letter from the police station in Singapore, and gather other documents listed in the acceptance form, some of which I managed to do while others I could not, simply because of time constraints. Time and time again, I had to correspond with YWAM Scotland when various issues popped up. It was an exhausting and intensive one week before the start of school, and I felt as though I was caught up in a whirlwind. I was trying my best to flow along with the circumstances, while not truly understanding what was actually happening, but living by faith and trusting God.

Then, there was still the problem of purchasing an airline ticket from Singapore to London. I had already bought a ticket from London to Scotland on Easyjet, so that I would arrive at the school on January 17. But if I couldn't get an airplane ticket to London on time, I would have to forgo the airline ticket to Scotland. I presented this problem to YWAM Scotland as well. It was then that they dropped a bombshell. The leaders had decided that I needed to arrive in Scotland by January 22 in order to be accepted by the school. Should I not be able to come by then, I would not be allowed to join the January 2004 DTS in Scotland. This was painful and shocking news to me. After all that I had already gone through, I still had to face the possibility that despite being accepted, I might not be able to attend because I could not catch a flight out of Singapore.

Up to that point in time, the school had provided information that was somewhat vague and not exactly explicit. Certain things were implied but not guaranteed, and my friends started asking me many questions. "Do the school fees include payment for everything? Where is the school located? Do you know how to get there? Do the people speak English? Do they provide food and accommodations? Are there any Asians? Is it safe to go there alone? Will you know anyone there?..." And I had no answers.

Obstacle after obstacle was before me, and I finally reached a point where I doubted it was God's will for me to go. I grew extremely discouraged because nothing seemed to be working right. Everything that could go wrong went wrong, and everything that could possibly happen, happened...and I had not even started school yet.

## Is This Really God's Will?

Then I told my sister that I didn't think it was God's will for me to go to Scotland. But yet, I knew that when we walk in God's plan, the enemy will come and do everything he can to prevent us from entering into our destiny, where we are supposed to be. He will try every trick up his sleeve, making it seem like it is not God's will, and make everything go horribly wrong and extremely difficult. He will attack you until you cannot take it anymore and until you give up. It is his tactic and will always remain one of his most powerful tactics. Indeed, what Dean Sherman says in his book, *Spiritual Warfare for Every Christian*, is so true:

> "It is this weapon of endurance [not giving up] that finally convinces the devil that he has to give up. Too many Christians quit minutes before the victory....
> We are a generation of quitters. We quit our places of leadership. We quit our marriages. We drop out of church....Don't we realize that this is part of the warfare?...The winner will always be the one who doesn't give up".[1]

When I told my sister that I didn't think it was God's will for me to go to Scotland, to my surprise, she insisted that I go. In fact, she declared that it was God's will for me to go, and she wholeheartedly supported me. I was amazed. Previously, two years before, she had been the person who vehemently objected to me going to the Discipleship Training School, and now, she was telling me that I needed to go, that it was God's will for me to go. Was I hearing correctly? My greatest opponent was now my strongest ally. Only God could have created this miracle.

It meant so much for to me to receive this support from my sister, knowing the financial strain that I was putting on her with my decision to attend DTS. Yet God had proved that He is my Jehovah Jireh. And this God who provides would surely remove every obstacle that stood in my way. He would open a way where there seemed to be no way, for nothing is impossible with God! He had brought me so far, not to leave me or forsake me, but to complete the good work that He had begun.

And so I continued to pray and trust God. And by God's grace, I finally was able to purchase an airline ticket from Singapore to London, traveling on January 20, 2004 via Malaysian Airlines and connecting with a corresponding flight from London to Scotland. A miracle had indeed happened, and I was on my way to a new adventure. The darkest and bleakest hours had come just before the answer. Although I would be a few days late for the start of school, I would still be arriving by God's grace, and in His time. It might have been a difficult and turbulent journey thus far, but surely God watched over me like He watches over all His creation. He makes all things beautiful in His time.

## ENDNOTE

1. Dean Sherman, *Spiritual Warfare for Every Christian*, Study Guide Edition (Seattle, WA: YWAM Publishing, 1995).

CHAPTER SEVEN

# *Heaven's Rain at a Castle in the Air*

The will of God is confirmed through *circumstances*.[1]

Jim W. Goll

*The Spirit of the Lord God is upon me; because the Lord hath anointed me to preach good tidings unto the meek; He hath sent me to bind up the brokenhearted, to proclaim liberty to the captives, and the opening of the prison to them that are bound; to proclaim the acceptable year of the Lord, and the day of vengeance of our God; to comfort all that mourn; to appoint unto them that mourn in Zion, to give unto them beauty for ashes, the oil of joy for mourning, the garment of praise for the spirit of heaviness... (Isaiah 61:1-3).*

## *My Journey in Scotland Begins*

F inally, on January 21, 2004 at noon, about a week after DTS started, I arrived at YWAM in Scotland. It had been an incredible trip thus far, and I had no idea that this was just the beginning of a journey that would change my life and my image of who God is.

I took a short rest followed by lunch, and then I was introduced to my schoolmates, many of whom called me immediately by name. Everyone else had already met each other. A little while later, I headed for bed as I had traveled almost nonstop from Singapore to London and then on to Scotland.

The next day, I was informed by one of the students that the school theme was Isaiah 61 and that our classroom was called "The Tent of Meeting." It was only after I completed the DTS program that I realized that for each DTS around the world, the leaders would pray before the start of the school, seeking God's agenda for that particular school. Isaiah 61 was not for every school, nor was every school's classroom called "The Tent of Meeting."

Twenty-five students from 14 nations were enrolled at our DTS. There were two students from Asia, namely Singapore and South Korea, among students from America, Finland, Switzerland, Norway, Germany, and the Netherlands. It was like a mini-United Nations, gathering together as one Body of Christ to seek God and know Him. The unity of the different nations coming together as one was a beautiful sight to behold and to be a part of.

Thus, I began my journey into a whole new world of Christianity, a world I had never entered before in the nearly two decades of my Christian walk. And for the very first time, I felt that this is what it must have been like to live in the days of Acts, to experience a new thing from God each day.

## *Am I Hearing From God?*

One of the first things we were taught was "Expect God to act; expect God to move." We needed to learn to expect God to come and move in our midst, to perform signs and wonders.

On my second day at the school, something amazing happened as we listened to a lesson on "How to Hear God Speak." Previously, some people had told me that God speaks, but I had never heard Him. I assumed that He spoke in an audible voice and I would be able to hear Him just like I can hear other people talk. But often, God speaks in a different way—into our hearts and our spirits. We hear Him, not in an audible voice, but in the soft whispers to our heart, in the gentle promptings to our spirits. However, we often fail to recognize His voice when He speaks to us in a gentle whisper, or we ignore the soft promptings of our heart.

On this day, the students were gathered in groups of three and seated together to pray for one another. I was sitting with two other students whom I had just met and knew absolutely nothing about. We quietened our hearts, spoke in tongues, and waited for God to speak. In a short time, a thought came to my mind—*brother and pain*—for one of the prayer partners, and I was taken aback. Had I heard correctly? Was this me, or was this God, or was this a devil? I didn't know this classmate or anything about her. So, I asked if she had a brother and whether he was in pain. She responded and said that indeed she had a brother who was in a lot of pain. This personal and specific word from God touched this classmate, and I was overwhelmed by what had happened. To me, this was a great miracle. Moreover, I was about to see, hear, and experience even more amazing things in the days ahead.

## In Awe of the Power of God

Everything at DTS was a surreal and unbelievable experience. God came so close and was so real that I could almost touch Him, and it was incredible to see Him move so powerfully during this short period of time. Indeed, He broke through every one of my areas of resistance and denial, and caused a huge paradigm shift in my life. I began to really believe that everything in the Bible is true, and every believer can live and walk in its reality right now on earth.

Worship times were more than worship—sometimes it was war-like with people wielding real swords and screaming "Freedom!" for the oppressed and captives. Some of the students worshipped and waved colorful banners with symbolic meanings, while others ran around the room like soldiers charging to war. It was highly intensive and extremely powerful. When I first experienced it, I was taken aback and quite frightened, as I had previously been accustomed to a dutifully quiet and sedate type of worship. I had never before felt such intensity of emotion in worship or seen such display of passion, anguish, and cries as people worshipped, praised, and prayed. After I left DTS, I realized that I missed such powerful sessions of passionate people coming together as one body with only one focus upon their minds—their love and passion for Jesus Christ.

Prayer sessions were more than simply prayers. I never realized that there were so many different ways and expressions, even in prayers. When we prayed for the nations, we often performed symbolic prophetic acts over the nations as led by the Holy Spirit. Sometimes, it was taking the soil of the land and prophesying over it; other times, it was pouring water over the land; and at yet other times, it was taking up a sword and declaring that we were fighting against the enemy. When we prayed for people, we went into the garden and asked God for a "word" or a "picture" for the person of what God wanted to tell them. When we prayed for each individual, we sometimes lifted up that person with our arms and proclaimed prophecies over their life. It was an amazing experience to live and learn daily in such a community.

Classes were always exciting, unusual, and full of surprises; and you never knew what to expect. I looked forward to every class with eager anticipation as the teachers allowed the Holy Spirit to flow freely and shared regarding what God had impressed upon their hearts in the areas of "Father, Heart of God," "Holy Spirit," "Spiritual Warfare," "Hearing God," and many other topics. During the week of "Destiny" teaching, our school leaders informed us that instead of inviting guest teachers or planning anything for the week, we would simply wait upon the Lord and follow the Holy Spirit's leading— which was so radically different from anything I've ever experienced or heard of in a class.

One of the most unforgettable things we did during this particular class was the prophetic act of "Crossing the Jordan River into the Promised Land." A symbolic blue cloth was laid on the floor in the class as a river. The students then laid down stones (with words written upon them of something we had asked God for). As a symbolic act, we picked up the individual stones and crossed the river to the other side to receive different things that had been placed upon a table. It was such a powerful session.

Over the next few months, we sat under many teachers. One of the lessons having the greatest impact was seeing the move of the prophetic in times of prayers and worship. In the traditional church, I had never been taught anything about the prophetic, but in DTS we lived and breathed the prophetic. I was to discover that God's gifts of the Holy Spirit in First Corinthians 12 had never ceased and are still very much alive this very day. Every so often, several of the different gifts were displayed right in the midst of a class, a prayer time, or a worship session. I had difficulty accepting what I was seeing with my eyes, and asked myself, *Is this possible? Are the gifts of the Holy Spirit still in existence in this age and time? How can I deny and refute them when I live in the very midst of them and am soaked in them continually? How can I say that this is not happening when all around me I see, feel, and hear testimony after testimony?*

I was blown away—blown away by God and what He was able to do, blown away by His awesomeness, majesty, and power. I had never seen a God like this. He was far bigger than I had imagined. Previously, I had put Him in a box and had limited His ability to move and act, simply because I had never experienced Him in the areas of the gifts of the Holy Spirit. Thus, because of my lack of experience, I had determined in my heart and agreed to the teachings that stated that God had ceased to move like He did in days gone by. My past beliefs, what and who I considered God to be, came crumbling down right before my very eyes.

God is so real; He is so close, but I had failed to see Him. I had been worshipping a wrong image of God, which had been planted in my heart and of which I was not even aware. I had even participated in condemning and critizing the charismatic churches, their doctrines, and teachings. And how wrong I had been. (Please forgive me, God, for my lack of knowledge and lack of faith.) But despite all that I had done, God in His mercy had directed me here and worked in a short six months to break down all the denials I had about the gifts of the Holy Spirit. My spirit eyes and ears were opened. For the very first time, I was beginning to have understanding like never before; I was having revelation like never before; I was having an experience of God like never before. And I didn't ever want to leave this place.

Indeed, the biggest impact must have been during the "Prophetic Track" when one of the YWAM staff taught us about prophetic acts and demonstrated them by performing a prophetic act on each of the ten students in this particular class. I had never spoken to her before, and neither had any one of the other students. Yet all the students were so amazed at how much time and effort she took to write three to five pages of prophetic words and knowledge about each of us. Each letter spoke to us personally about things we could relate to. Mine included symbolic words about my past, my hurts, my pain, and the valley of weeping I had gone through. Another student who grew up as a pastor's son received a summary of all the prophecies that had been spoken over his life. It blew my mind to think that someone who had never met me before, never knew about my past, was able to accurately write and talk about me. Indeed, each letter was different, but accurate. And if it was not of God, then who was it of? Where did it come from? Only God knows our past intimately—what we have gone through and walked through. I had never believed in the prophetic or people being able to truly hear from God, but when you see it happening with your own eyes and hear it with your own ears, how can you continue to not believe? How do you not see the reality of your faith, the goodness of God, or the bigness of God? I cried and cried when I read the letter she wrote to me. I felt as though it was God Himself speaking to me.

## Lessons Learned

The many lessons I learned in Scotland during those short months were a mind-blowing experience, some of which are as follows.

1. It's all about choices—my choices and the decisions I make. I need to choose to be holy. I need to choose to forgive. I need to choose to rise above tiredness. I need to choose not to give up. I need to choose God's will over my own desires. Every single believer has choices to constantly make. Will we make the right choice? Will we choose for God, or will we choose for ourselves and our selfish desires? (See Joshua 24:15.)

2. I need to learn to spend quality time with people and have meaningful conversations with them. Ask them how they feel. Ask them about their emotions. Ask them for their opinions. Be interested in them and show them that I care. Life is not just about me; it's about others and their feelings. I need to seek to understand others instead of wanting to be understood by others. (See Galatians 5:14.)

3. I need to consciously activate my spirit man to worship, to pray, to read the Bible (see 1 Cor. 14:14-15), to seek the Lord, to do His will, to hear His voice. I must expand the effort to act, to do, and to live. Nothing ventured, nothing gained. For everything that we receive, there is a price to pay. If I am not willing to pay the price and make the effort, how can I expect to receive?

4. I need to learn what it means to be a "passionate" Christian. I think about all the YWAM-ers around me during the short six months in DTS, and I am amazed at their passion for God, their faith, their desire to know God at a deeper level, their willingness to give up everything for Jesus Christ, for the sake of the cross. How many of us are willing to give up even a tiny thing like comfort, security, title, salary for the sake of the cross, and follow Christ no matter where He leads, even if it means the jungles of Ecuador? (See Matthew 16:24.) I cannot imagine the price that great men and women throughout history have paid to know God deeply and intimately, the untold stories of hundreds and thousands of martyrs who have died in China, India, and many other parts of the world.

5. I need to *expect God to act* (see Isa. 64:3-4). Expect great things from God, expect God to keep His word, expect God to move, expect God to speak. If we don't expect, how can we receive? God's words and promises do not return to Him void, but will fulfill everything that He speaks forth.

6. *Humility* is very important in our Christian walk. It is the key to a greater and better service for our Lord and King. He desires to see a humble heart in me. I need to consider others better than myself, not just in speech and in action, but also in my heart towards others (see Phil. 2:3).

7. The Bible, God's Word, is the supreme *Truth* in my life. I should trust, believe, and hope for everything that the Bible says with regard to all things, including who I am in Christ, God's undying love for me, what I need to do, and the life I need to live as a Christian. We

need to learn to be not merely readers of the Word, but doers of the Word (see James 1:22). We need to allow the Word of God, which is active, like a double-edged sword, to divide our soul and spirits; and live in holy, reverent fear of the Lord (see Heb. 4:12).

8. I have *authority* over demonic and evil forces. Jesus died and He rose again, giving me back the authority God ordained me to have as a person on earth when I accepted Jesus Christ as my Lord and Savior. I need to exercise this authority that I have been given in order to set myself and others free—free from the bondages, lies, darkness, strongholds, and deceptions that the devil has built in the life of believers and non-believers. We wrestle not against flesh and blood but against principalities and powers of darkness (see Eph. 6:12). But we have already won because Christ has died, and He has risen victorious. We need to let this truth sink into our hearts and claim the victory that is already ours.

9. There is great *power* in the Holy Spirit, and I need to call on this power to carry me through (see Zech. 4:6). What I cannot do, God *can* do by the empowerment of the Holy Spirit. Nothing is impossible. I need to activate my spirit, speak in tongues, and communicate with God spirit to spirit. True worshippers worship in spirit and in truth (see John 4:23).

10. It's okay not to know my future, my destiny, or what is ahead, for God knows and He will lead and provide at just the right time. I only need to rest and trust in His character. He has promised in His Word that He knows the plans He has for each and every one of us, plans to prosper us and not to harm us, plans to give us a hope and a future (see Jer. 29:11).

11. Spiritual warfare in the unseen realm is very real, and my role in the battle is to take my sword, which is the Word of God, and fight for the freedom of myself and others through worship, intercession, and declaration of who God is. The invisible realm is as real if not more so than the physical. It has existed for eons and will continue to exist for eternity, whereas what is seen is temporary (see 2 Cor. 4:18).

12. God's timing is perfect. He knew exactly when to bring me to DTS and where I should go. He knows what I need and always provides at the right time, even when I might think otherwise. God's timing is different from man's timing, and I need to understand that He makes all things beautiful in His time, not my time (see Eccl. 3:11).

13. I have learned to hear God's voice and that God does speak to me, if only I will listen to Him, if only I will trust that still small Voice who wants to be heard. How many of us spend adequate time, sitting, waiting, listening, and asking God to speak to us? And how many of us expect God to speak? Even after completing DTS, I am still guilty of not spending enough time to hear from God. If I don't listen, how can I hear? (See John 10:14-16.)

14. Character and anointing must go hand in hand. If there is a gap between these two, you are bound to fall and fail. We need to first mold our character in order to do the work that God has anointed us to do, for our anointing can only be as high as our character. If our anointing is stronger than our character, sooner or later, our character will bring the anointing to the place of our character. We must have right character in order to move in the anointing that God has for us.

Without character, there cannot be a corresponding level of anointing (see 1 Sam. 15:21–16:14).

## The Reasons God Brought Me to Scotland

After DTS ended, I asked God why He brought me all the way to Scotland, halfway across the world, to do my DTS when I could have completed it just as easily in Singapore.

He said that He loves me and that He always listens to all my prayers. He knows what I love and what my desires and dreams are. His desire is to give me the best there is, but sometimes my desires are not good for me; hence, He loves me too much to grant my desires. Other times, I do not receive the desires of my heart because the time is not right. God makes all things beautiful in His time.

Several years earlier, I had gone to Europe on a tour after my graduation and was scheduled to tour Scotland, but because my grandmother fell critically ill, I had to terminate my trip at London and return home to Singapore. It was then that I told God that one day, I would come back to Scotland; but never in my wildest imagination did I think that God would bring me back to Scotland to do my DTS. I had forgotten even this promise that I made to myself, but God did not forget. During that same trip after graduation, I had toured much of Europe but had been greatly disappointed to have not visited even one castle, despite the fact that there are hundreds of castles all over Europe. We had run out of time. I told God then that I wanted very much to visit a castle and perhaps even stay in one.

When I went to Scotland to complete my DTS, I never expected to end up living in a castle-like building that houses more than 100 people. It sits on a little hill overlooking the most beautiful sea and sunset that anyone could imagine. Looking out one of the windows of our school, there is the most breathtaking view in the world. I was living in a castle in the air, surrounded by glen and hills, rolling seas, and beautiful pastures. God then revealed to me that He had led me to this particular school because He knew that I loved the sea, and this castle was situated five minutes away from the most awesome beach and sea one can imagine.

God then went on to tell me that He knew my fascination with foreigners and making friends from foreign countries. Hence, He directed me to a school where I was one of the two students from Asia amongst others from America and Europe—a school made up of people from more than 14 nations around the world.

I was overwhelmed by God's love and goodness to me. For years, I had been a Christian, but there were many times that I could not feel God's presence and did not think that God cared about me or knew anything about me. He often seemed absent when I needed Him most and did not seem to hear any of my prayers, let alone answer them. I had spent hours crying out to Him but there was not a word from Him in response. My prayers had often been met with silence, and you can imagine my shock when I ended up in a school that I had no intention of enrolling in, in a country I had not planned to go, to only find a God I had never met before. For the very first time in my life, God was so real; I felt I could touch Him. He was so close, and He knew me so deeply and intimately that it shocked me. I was taken aback by this marvelous and wonderfully loving God. Indeed, Graham Cooke is right when He says, "God hides for a reason—so that He can develop you on the inside and train you to see with eyes of faith. In manifestation, you can already see what God is doing."[2] When He manifests Himself, we as believers are often in awe of God and it becomes more like a dream.

Then, God reminded me of something I had said to a friend after he scaled the Himalayan Mountains a few years back. Looking at his photos, I was amazed at the beauty of this mountain range, and I made a decision that I would climb the Himalayan Mountains one day and that I would do it before I was 30 years old. Subsequently, while attending DTS, God made all my dreams, desires, and thoughts become a reality. Indeed, while in Scotland I went to India and to the Himalayan Mountains as part of my outreach to the nations. I had not intended to go to India, neither had I made any plans to climb the Himalayan Mountains, but God being God often brings surprises when He comes. I climbed the Himalayan Mountains a few months before I turned the age of 30.

This DTS experience was a dream come true—living in a castle, meeting people from all over the world who are passionate about God, and climbing the Himalayan Mountains. What more could I have asked for?

## Heaven's Rain

I felt as though I was under a heavy rain shower of God during my time at Scotland. Heaven's rain poured down upon me, and it washed away all the bad experiences of the past, all the pain, and all the disillusionment; and in its place was everything that God wanted to give in order to bless me—His love, His tenderness, His grace, His mercy, in accordance with the prophecy that was spoken over me:

> *See, the rain is falling over you. You may feel it already*
> *or not yet. But My Spirit is falling over you, upon you;*
> *and the rain is increasing and becoming more and more*

*intense. I make your valley of Baka* [Hebrew: weeping]
*a place of springs, and the rains cover it with pools* [Hebrew: blessings] *(see Psalm 84:6). I am making your
valley of Achor* [Hebrew: trouble], *a door of hope (see
Hosea 2:15)....For you are under the rain of My Spirit.*

I pray that even as you read this book, this rain that is
falling over me (the rain of God's Spirit) would fall over you as
well. I pray that Heaven's rain will fall over your life and over
all that you are going through. I pray that there will be a
cleansing and a blessing far beyond what you can comprehend, and that all your valleys of Baka and Achor would become a place of springs and blessings.

## ENDNOTES

1. Jim W. Goll, *The Beginner's Guide to Hearing God* (Ventura, CA: Regal, 2004).

2. Graham Cooke, *When the Lights Go Out* (Grand Rapids, MI: Chosen, 2003), 26-27.

## CHAPTER EIGHT

# Who Is My Neighbor?

Jesus left His home, He let go of His rights in Heaven. If we are to follow His example, we need to let go of our home, our culture, our family and friends, and all that is precious and important to us because of *a higher calling.*[1]

Floyd McClung

*How then shall they call on Him in whom they have not believed? and how shall they believe in Him of whom they have not heard? and how shall they hear without a preacher? And how shall they preach, except they be sent? as it is written, How beautiful are the feet of them that preach the gospel of peace, and bring glad tidings of good things!* (Romans 10:14-15)

## Touched by the People of India

Together with six other students and two team leaders, nine of us left Scotland and traveled to the vast nation of India, while other DTS students journeyed to Morocco, Turkey, or remained in Scotland.

Before traveling to India, however, we attended sessions where people from India, or who had been to India, came and shared with us some of the things that we would probably face while ministering there, including the cultural shock, the various colors, the smells, the poverty, and the different lifestyles. But even these warnings were not enough to equip us for what we would encounter in this needy country. Although we had been prepared mentally, we were still overwhelmed when we came face-to-face with the reality in India. All five of our senses were assaulted—sight, the smell, the noise, the taste, and the touch. Yet it was not all bad—just different and often difficult.

India does have her charms, but it is also a very painful experience. The poverty that surrounds you daily is heartbreaking, especially while knowing that you cannot do much about it. There is a great, uncrossable divide between the wealthy and the poor, and everywhere we turned, there were beggars young and old asking for food or money. We did not have much money, but what we had, we gave. It was through this experience that I composed my very first poem. I felt unable to verbally describe my feelings and emotions resulting from what I saw, yet I wanted to share this experience with my friends. Consequently, the following poem was birthed.

When I walk on the streets of Delhi, what do I see?
A man cycling a rickshaw carrying two big passengers;

A woman with a baby reaching out her hands for help;
A child, naked and hungry, waiting to be fed;
A lame man struggling to move ahead;
A blind man being led by the staff in his hands;
A man with no hands asking for alms.

When I see the people in Delhi, what do I do?
I reach out my hand and give to the poor;
I send His message of love and look into their eyes;
I give them my food, my money, my tears;
I give them the love of Jesus and give them my ears;
I respond with my eyes, my heart, my hands;
I reach out and touch them with the Father's love.

Now that I have done all that I can,
where will these people go on from here?
Strangers will come and give them their food;
Strangers will come and give them their money;
Strangers will come and take away their pain;
Strangers will come and show them the way;
Strangers will come and give them hope for a new day;
Strangers like me, like you, and everyone else who can.

How can anyone go to a nation like India and not feel the pain of the Father's heart while witnessing misery of His beloved children? No one can go to India and return to their nation unaffected by the suffering that these people bear. Then I ask, who is my neighbor? He is the one who needs my help, the one whom I can stretch my hand out to and give what I can. Perhaps it's just a little love, a little touch, a little money, or a little heart. But that little, if given by many people, can be combined together to touch lives and change destinies.

Although my trip to India was only a short three months, that time left a dent in my life, and something was deposited in me—a new compassion for the poor and people in need. Living in Singapore where there is much prosperity, I have always had everything I need and want, and there is seldom any lack. Most citizens own their homes and can afford to travel. They possess televisions, phones, computers, and other conveniences. Compared to India, I live in the lap of luxury. There are poor people who live in Singapore too; but the government helps these people in various ways, and their plight is not as stark as the destitute who barely survive on the streets of India. Traveling from a nation like Singapore to Scotland had been a relatively easy transition because the standards of living are similar as is the way of life, which I often take for granted. But the transition from Singapore and Scotland to India was difficult. We had to deal with problems involving just basic necessities, like going to the toilet and not having toilet paper, using pails instead of a shower, and eating with our hands instead of with utensils.

Yet despite the difficulties we encountered daily, India has many charms. It is such a colorful nation, and people are generally friendly. In fact, at times, their hospitality is astounding. They will treat you like an honored guest and serve you with their best tea and snacks. Visiting some of the marketplaces was a visual treat. The array and variety of spices, fruits, and saris were fascinating to behold. In addition, our tastebuds were challenged and stretched when we tried the multitude of flavors and spices.

## The Streets and Gates of India

While in India, our team was involved in many different types of work. We visited the slums and provided basic healthcare to the people—simple things like cutting their nails and hair. We also befriended the children and tried our best to spread the love of God in their hearts. We played with them, performed skits, and taught them songs and crafts.

We also befriended the porters who live in the railway stations. These porters have no homes and often no food. They earn a living by carrying heavy loads for passengers who travel from one city to another via the Indian railway. They are often ostracized and treated as outcasts by their fellow countrymen. We talked with them, played and laughed with them, praying that these little acts would help make them feel special. We reached out to them and shared God's love with them.

YWAM India had a coffeehouse where we performed Christian rock music, skits, and dances for the young, hippy Indian crowd. Every week while visiting this coffeehouse, we led worship, performed, or just chatted with the youth. We held evangelistic events and shared Jesus with them in ways that they could relate to.

Before the teams had left Scotland to go to the various nations around the world, we gathered as a school and prayed for each team. We had a time of "commissioning" by the Scotland YWAM base leadership to send us forth to the nations. At one point, someone gave a prophetic word to the India team. She saw a picture of iron gates and the team with heads down, wondering how we could go through this gate. Then one of the members came, pushed the gates, and the doors swung open. A word was given that "God will open a way, and we do not have to be afraid of any gate because they will open!" Never did the India team expect to find that when we reached India, one of our weekly tasks would be to pray for the gates of the city to be opened, for God to come into the city and transform the city, as well as for the Gospel to go out from the city to the rest of India. It was amazing to see that what had been spoken of, with no foreknowledge by anyone in Scotland, would come to pass in India.

The YWAM-ers in India had been praying for the past four years for the gates of this particular city to be opened, and it was the first time that a team from Scotland YWAM had gone into this city. They had a revelation from God about praying for the gates of the city, but they had no idea where the gates were located. After some time, the local newspaper published a map of the city showing all the gateways to and from the city. Without fail, the people had been praying every Saturday from 6:00 A.M. to 10:00 A.M. at every gate of the city. We joined in the effort, but it was difficult praying weekly. There was one week when we all were particularly discouraged and had no strength to go on. Then one of the team members stood to encourage us and remind us that we were there to fight, and fight we must. At that moment, I could see the prophecy in action, as this very person had been named in the picture that was given to us while we were in Scotland. It was awesome to be involved in something so small, yet so significant.

Also, on a weekly basis, we visited various churches all around the city where we led worship and the team leaders shared the Word of God. The students also took turns, sharing testimonies and performing skits and dances at the churches.

We also knocked on doors, visited households, and befriended the local Indians. We went shopping with them, watched movies with them, ate with them, and laughed with them. Even as we befriended them, in all ways possible, we tried to show them the God we believed in and prayed that they too would come to know Him and be transformed.

We fasted and prayed for the nation of India for her salvation, for her eyes to be opened to the Gospel, and for the light of God to shine in this nation filled with darkness. We spoke God's Word over the nation and proclaimed and declared God's mercy upon this land. We performed prophetic acts as we interceded for this land and cried out to God to have compassion on her people and rescue them.

We organized youth camps for the believers in the Indian churches, teaching them everything that we ourselves learned and poured our hearts into the lives of the future leaders and pillars of the Indian Church. We prayed for them to receive the baptism of the Holy Spirit. We taught them that God still speaks today and informed them of what they needed to do in order to hear His voice and know His heartbeat. We reminded them of the price Jesus Christ paid for them, led them through a time of commitment to God, and encouraged them to partake in the Great Commission and do their part to reach the world for Jesus.

## *"Oh, God, Help India!"*

But whatever we did seemed so insignificant and appeared to be just a drop in the ocean. India has a population of more than one billion, which means that every sixth person on the earth is an Indian. Furthermore, theirs is a nation seeped in idolatry, a nation who knows not the God of Israel. At last count, they have more than three million gods. They worship anything and everything from cows to pop stars. Shrines are erected everywhere. If you tell them about the love of Jesus Christ for them, they might accept Jesus as their Lord and Savior, but they often do not accept Him as their one and only God and Savior. They will accept Jesus Christ as one of the many gods that they worship. They are a holy and god-fearing people. They will anoint everything they have and seek blessing even for their vehicles in their Hindu temples. So, how do we spread the love of God into a nation that is seeped in religious beliefs, that sometimes burns Christians who dare to enter their territory to share the message of God's love, where certain states have outlawed conversion to Christianity and convict offenders with the death penalty, and where Christians' lives are at risk simply because of their religious beliefs?

Only God can do something for this nation; only the prayers of the saints reaching to Heaven can change the state of this nation; only those who dedicate their lives to this nation can see God's heartbeat for this nation in the midst of the gloom and darkness. Who can stop the husbands from burning their wives, from burying their wives alive, from aborting hundreds of thousands of unborn baby girls? Who can stop the acts of cruelty and lawlessness that are often hidden by the media? No one...except God.

Oh God, have mercy and compassion on the Indians. They know not what they are doing. They have no wisdom, no insight about the love of God. Open their eyes that they may see. Open their minds that they may comprehend. Open their ears that they may hear the good news of the Gospel and receive salvation. Open their hearts that they may receive the love of God that transcends all understanding!

India is our neighbor. She is part of our world, part of us. Let us extend our hands and reach out to this nation who is crying out to God to help her. She is drowning under the acts of lawlessness, the injustice towards the various castes, and cruelty to the poor. Can we hear the cry of this nation? Can we do something to help? Oh God, send Your help to this nation.

Thank You for the miracles we have heard and seen, for the people who have experienced miraculous healings, who were delivered from the hands of the enemy, who had a revelation of God. God, let there be an increase of Your power witnessed in this nation in this last hour. Hear the desperate needs and cries of Your children here on earth and come and rescue them.

## *Up the Himalayan Mountains*

With a heavy heart, our team left the city and climbed the mountains of Himalaya—this great mountain range famous for its ancient Hindu temples and shrines, where thousands upon thousands gather yearly to worship, where 99 percent of the people are committed, strong-believing Hindus, and almost every household has an altar where daily worship is performed. Spiritual darkness prevails in thousands of villages, and there are very few Christians in this remote part of the world.

Yet eternity has been planted by God into the hearts of men, and God's truth has been revealed to all men through creation (see Eccl.; Rom. 1:20). And so, men are without excuse, including the Indians. Those who have not heard of God will be without excuse at the day of judgment, because God has put eternity in every man's heart.

Up in the mountainous villages and ranges, we spent our days praying. For a few weeks, we interceded for this unreached people group; and as we stood in the gap, it was often difficult to pray. We were tired, exhausted, and hoarse from praying non-stop, day in and day out. People were there who had prayed for more than a decade and not seen much fruit; in fact, the number of lives who were transformed could be counted with their ten fingers after more than a decade. Still they went on, still they continued, still they preserved, still they did not give up.

And so, how could we give up when we had been there for only a few short weeks? We scaled the great Himalayan

Mountains and prayed. It was a physically (carrying full backpacks uphill), spiritually (waking up at 6:00 A.M. daily to pray for the Indians before climbing), mentally (forcing ourselves to go on when our entire bodies were screaming in pain), and emotionally (trying hard not to be left behind and feeling horrible to be the last man to always reach base camp, often hours later than the first man) challenging experience. I often felt like giving up along the way. It was almost too much for me to bear. But I learned some very important spiritual lessons even in this trek.

One day at about lunchtime, I felt very hungry and tired after a particularly steep uphill climb, and lunch was still nowhere in sight. Then one of the guides gave me something to eat to boost my strength. Although it was just a small piece of biscuit, I felt so good after eating it, and I found that I was totally refreshed and energized. I felt that God was teaching me a spiritual lesson. As Christians, we can do so much work as we serve the church, attend Bible studies, pray, intercede, worship, and serve as ushers. These services or ministries are like climbing up a mountain, and after a long period of time can become very tiring so that we want to give up and let go of our responsibilities. We then need to eat the biscuits, to get refreshment from the Holy Spirit in order to carry on, or else we will burn out and not have energy to continue on.

## Running and Finishing the Race

At the end of the trek, as we came down from the Himalayan Mountains, I had yet another revelation. Every day, I had been the last person to reach the campsite, which had been very discouraging. But God reminded me that it's like my Christian walk. It's not how fast or how slow our journey is. It's about completing the trek, completing the race. It's not how well you start or how well you perform during your lifetime. It's about whether you can complete the race. It's about whether you remain a Christian until the very end, no matter what difficulties or obstacles you face. Some Christians start well, and during their lifetime, they achieve remarkable success and do great exploits for God. But during the last leg, because of pride or enticements of the devil, they fall away from God and leave the Christian faith. It's not just about doing well during the race—it's about completing the race.

The Christians we met on the Himalayan Mountains showed us what it means to pray and to believe God even when there is no visible signs of an answer in the physical realm. They showed us what it means to run the race and push on even when it is hard and difficult. They showed us what true perseverance is in the face of difficulty. They showed us what true love is. Many of them had uprooted themselves from their nations and homes and had come to India to call these people their own. They loved them, and they learned their language and culture. They wore their clothes, ate their food, and planted themselves in their midst. They are nameless and faceless people in the Christian world, but they are known by God because of their love for His children, because they are not afraid and they fight on, often in small groups of less than ten.

The fact is that less than 10 percent of the missionaries around the world work among this unreached people group. One percent of the gifts given by the church are given for the work among the unreached people groups. Ninety-four percent of the church funds are used for church buildings and local ministries. We might not know whether we are called to be a "goer" (to go into the nations) or a "sender" (to send goers into the nations), but we can still be a light to the nations, to the unreached people groups. Both are important to God.

Let us be faithful to the calling that God has for each of us, and let us be involved wherever we are until we are certain that we are called to be a "goer." Until that day comes, let us commit ourselves to be "senders." Let us give our resources to send others out to the nations. Let us support them in prayers and petitions, in finances, in encouragement, in practical help, and in blessings. No gift is too small, and no effort is too little in the Kingdom of God. Every little drop of rain counts. And one day, all the drops of rain will be gathered together to become a huge ocean—an ocean so big that no one will be able to resist it. And when that day comes, our Lord Jesus Christ will come in all His glory and splendor and gather us up together with Him to the new Heaven and new Earth to spend eternity with Him.

## ENDNOTE

1. Floyd McClung, *Spirits of the City* (Eastbourne, UK: Kingsway Communications, 1990).

CHAPTER NINE

# Is There a Demon in Me?

We are *seekers* of God, not the enemy.[1]

Graham Cooke

*And these signs shall follow them that believe; in My name shall they cast out devils; they shall speak with new tongues; they shall take up serpents; and if they drink any deadly thing, it shall not hurt them; they shall lay hands on the sick, and they shall recover (Mark 16:17-18).*

## Time to Return Home

After the amazing six months of DTS, of which three months were spent in Scotland and three months spent in India, I knew in my heart that the real reason why I first left Singapore for London was to eventually attend DTS in the country of God's choice.

Thereafter, the need and desire to work in London disappeared, and I knew that I had to return to Singapore. I did not know why, but in the end, I realized that it was God's abundant mercy and grace that led me back to Singapore. If I had stayed on in London to work and then return two years later as originally planned, it would probably have been to attend my sister's funeral, and I would have regretted it for the rest of my life. God in His mercy knew the future and brought me back to Singapore to spend the remaining years of my sister's life with her. Every so often, we realize God's love and mercy in our life, but not until many years after an event has occurred. My sister's death, of course, is another story and another chapter.

Life is full of ups and downs, yet through it all we need to see God and His hand at work in our lives, even though sometimes, it is very difficult to do so. Sometimes He appears to be very distant and aloof, and it seems that He does not care whether we live or die.

At one point, He seemed to have disappeared from my life completely. Yet at other times, He came in His majestic power, and I was taken aback by His splendor, His knowledge, His wisdom, His greatness, and His love for me. We often hover between two images or experiences of God in our life. More often than not, He chooses to disguise Himself and seems to hide Himself so that we cannot see or feel Him. But He is still there. He is still the same, even though why or how He manifests Himself might remain a mystery. He is God. We can cry, we can shout, we can scream, we can long, we can be in agony, and yet still He refuses to show up. Why? Because He is God.

All sovereignty belongs to Him. He says I will have mercy on whom I will have mercy (see Exod. 33:19b).

Upon my return to Singapore, I left my previous traditional church and joined a charismatic church. It was difficult leaving my church where many people could not understand my decision, but I knew in my heart that I had to move on. If I stayed on, I would not grow. There were too many questions and too many issues that I needed to learn more about. If I stayed on, who would explain to me or talk to me about demons, speaking in tongues, the gifts of the Holy Spirit, such as word of knowledge, word of wisdom, and prophecy? No one in the traditional church talked about such things. We knew that there are angels and demons; we knew that there are gifts of the Holy Spirit, but we had no understanding or revelation. Moreover, there were often many arguments about various teachings that were never resolved. Yet I needed to learn and grow.

## Demons in Christians?

After joining a charismatic church, I also joined a cell group. At times, the church taught on spiritual warfare, and if there was anyone who was demonized or suspected to be demonized, they were brought to these sessions. Subsequently, the pastors, in front of everyone, would demonstrate how to cast out demons.

This practice was very new and strange to me. I had heard much about demons and casting out demons, but had never really seen it done before this time. After witnessing demons expelled from certain people, I began to see clearly that even in this day and age, there really is such a thing as being demonized. But the existence of demons still did not have much impact on me.

Then one day in my cell group, I learned that one of the members who had been a Christian for many years had a legion

EVERY BELIEVER'S GUIDE TO THE SUPERNATURAL

(numbered between 4,200 to 6,000 soldiers) cast out from her. It was a shock to me as I had been taught that only non-Christians could be possessed by demons. How could a person who had been saved, baptized in water, baptized with the Holy Spirit, and had spoken in tongues need to be delivered from a demon? This was a new doctrine to me and one that I could not understand. I asked several questions. *Can this be true? Is it really possible that Christians can have demons in them that need to be driven out?* I was very confused and talked to two of my very close friends about it. To my surprise, they agreed that it was possible, and they told me that they themselves had demons previously cast out from them. This was shocking news, especially because I had known them for many years but never knew that such a thing had happened to them. My mind was in a whirl, trying to process all the new information I was receiving. Yet, still I decided not to pursue or conduct any further research.

Consequently, I was not prepared for what happened a few months after learning that Christians can be oppressed by demons. I would come face-to-face with the demons in my own life.

## Demons of My Own

The possibility that I could be under the influence of a demon never crossed my mind, especially since I had been a Christian for many years. Like many other Christians, I tried hard to be a good person and live a godly life. I had sinned against God in my word, my thoughts, my speech, and my actions; but whenever I sinned, I would confess my sins and repent and try my utmost to not sin again. For sure, I had struggled with many issues in my life, as do many Christians, but at no point in time did I suspect that anything could have led to a demon entering me. The thought was just so impossible and so unimaginable.

Then one day, I attended a Christian camp where I was totally unprepared for the manifestation of a demon in me. Nothing happened during the first two days, but on the third day during a worship session, I started to feel like I had to vomit. Then I started to cough. It was a normal cough at first, but then it became abnormal and intense; and I found myself in a posture in which I could not move any part of my body. My hands were numb, and I was aware of all my surroundings; but I could not move at all. It was as though someone or something had taken over my body, and I was no longer in control or in charge. I wanted to scream for help, but no voice came out. I just could not do anything.

Then I became conscious of the pastors coming to me and praying over me, and I was back to normal again. In a state of shock, I wondered what this was all about and how I could be possessed by a demon. I was terrified and extremely confused. It was one thing to hear and read about demons manifesting in others and being cast out, but a totally different matter to have it happen to me. In fact, it was unthinkable. What if there were more demons in me that needed to be cast out? What should I do?

## Overcoming Demons by the Blood of Jesus Christ

And so, I went for counseling with the pastors of my new church. I also went to healing and deliverance sessions. I did not know what to expect in these sessions, and I was already freaked out by what had happened during the camp. I was still such a baby in the spiritual realm although I had been a

Christian for many years—it had been less than a year that I was baptized in the Holy Spirit and speaking in tongues. The pastor had told me that sometimes we engage ourselves in the wrong battles and end up fighting a losing war. For example, we might try to battle and bind spiritual strongholds within, when in fact, the battle is in the spiritual environment. I learned that I needed to build myself up in the Word of God to be sure of my identity and my authority in Christ Jesus. Our authority over demons is solely from the victory that Jesus Christ won for us by the blood that He shed for our sins, His death on the cross, and His victorious resurrection. We as believers overcome satan and his demons by the blood of the Lamb and by the word of our testimony (see Rev. 12:11).

We cast out demons from ourselves and from others in the name of Jesus Christ and by the Word of God. The enemy is a defeated one, but still he will do everything he can to deceive Christians into believing that he has a hold and a power over their lives. He will not give up and will not stop deceiving. He is a liar and the father of lies (see John 8:44).

Yes, we all have sinned and have fallen short of the glory of God (see Rom. 3:23), but we must stop believing all the negative accusations that satan the accuser (see Rev. 12:10) hurls at us. The Bible is very clear on that. Whether the sin is big or small, a sin is a sin, and the wages of sin is death. But the Bible also says that the gift of God is eternal life through Jesus Christ our Lord and Savior (see Rom. 6:23). If we confess with our mouth and believe in our hearts that Jesus Christ is Lord, we are saved (see Rom. 10:9). There is no condemnation in Christ Jesus (see Rom. 8:1). We need to believe every word that the Bible says and rebuke every lie and every thought that the enemy plants in our heads. We need to reject the thoughts that we are not good enough, that because we are sinners it is no use, that we will never climb out of the sin. These are lies from the pit. God knows that we are sinners, but Christ became a curse for us so that we may have His life (see Rom. 3:13-14). If we sin, we need to confess to God that we have sinned and to repent of our sins and seek forgiveness.

I also learned through counseling that deliverance from demons sometimes happens over a period of time as I feed on God's Word. However, if I have sought counseling for demons to be expelled from me and nothing happens, then I need to believe that there is nothing in me and that whatever it was in me has gone. I should not continue to dwell on finding a demon in me—that was not what I was created for. I was created for God, to worship Him and Him alone. We are seekers of God, not the enemy. If there is a demon in me and it manifests, then I need to deal with it and cast it out. If there is nothing, then I do not need to continue to search for the demon. In any case, we should not worry about the manifestations of the demons; instead, we need to trust that our God is bigger than all these things and that I can overcome any demon by the blood of Jesus Christ.

As I feed on God's Word and the Holy Spirit fills me, whatever is not of God will have to leave. It is like a bottle of dirty water. I am the bottle, and the dirty water is my life of sin. As I put the bottle under a running tap of clear and clean water (the Word of God and the work of the Holy Spirit in my life), the running water will start to fill the bottle of dirty water. The bottle will overflow, and the dirty water will come out. It happens over a period of time. As more running water comes in, more dirty water goes out. Soon, all the dirty water will go out of the bottle, and only the clear and clean running water will remain. In the same way, as the Word of God and the Holy Spirit fills me (the bottle), the devil and the flesh (dirty water) will be purged out. Over a period of time, I will become clean and sanctified. However, sometimes in the process, I or someone else might pour dirty water in the bottle again. Hence, the running water needs to be constantly running and constantly filling the bottle; if not, the body will remain dirty.

## More About Demons

I started to read a lot of books, seeking understanding on this whole new area that I never thought was in existence in this present day. I now recommend two excellent books that give a clear understanding of how demons enter someone and how to be delivered and stay delivered. These two books are *Pigs in the Parlor* by Frank and Ida Mae Hammond, and *They Shall Expel Demons* by Derek Prince.

I began to understand that demons are unclean or evil spirits, and to be demonized is to be subject to demonic influence; it is not possession or ownership by the demons. Demons are spirits that have an intense craving to occupy physical bodies. If human beings are not available, they will enter the body of animals. This can be seen in the story of the demonized man at the Gerasenes. Jesus cast out the demons from him and allowed them to enter into pigs (see Luke 8:27-33). Demons can already be in a person before he becomes a Christian, or demons can enter a person after he becomes a Christian. If demons enter a person before he becomes a Christian, they do not automatically leave the person after he accepts Jesus Christ as Lord and Savior. They still need to be cast out.

Demons can enter a person through open doors once given an opportunity. They gain entrance through sins of commission, such as adultery, fornification, hatred, envy, murder, drunkenness, acupuncture, worship of idols, yoga, and marital arts; or through sins of omission, such as when a person fails to forgive, which opens the door to hatred and other related spirits. Demons can also enter a person through life circumstances, often during a person's childhood. They are no respecter of persons nor are they righteous, so given any chance they will enter a person. For example, a child might be a victim of a bad accident where he sees a lot of people die in front of him, and the demon of death might enter him. Or a child is not wanted because he has been born out of wedlock, or the family might have been too poor to keep him, so the spirit of rejection enters him. Demons can also enter by inheritance or a generational curse where a mother or father is schizophrenic. Consequently, the demons will choose one or more of the children to enter who will also become schizophrenic.

However, no demon can attack us or enter us unless it has an opening to do so. Fear can provide such an opening. We must not be afraid, and we must not give the demons any foothold or opening through which to enter. We must stand on the promise of Jesus' words that He has given us authority to trample on snakes and scorpions and to overcome all the power of the enemy; nothing will harm us (see Luke 10:19). The power and authority has already been given to us, and we need to exercise that authority. Otherwise, the authority will remain useless. It is like the police who have the authority to catch thieves and bring them to judgment, but if they just look at him committing the crime, the authority that the police have is useless. It is good for nothing.

## Steps to Deliverance and Retaining Deliverance

In their books, Frank and Ida Mae Hammond as well as Derek Prince provide guidelines or steps that you can take to lead you through deliverance. Some of these steps include personally affirming your faith in Jesus Christ. He is the only one through whom you can be set free from all demonic influences and strongholds in your life. If the Son of God sets you free, you will be free indeed (see John 8:36). In His name and His alone you can have victory over your sins and struggles. Nothing is impossible for Him.

We also need to humble ourselves before God and recognize that we are dependent on Him and His provision for deliverance. Without His help, no one can be delivered. We need to confess any known sins and bring these sins from darkness into light. When they are in the light, the accuser can no longer condemn and accuse us in the dark. Indeed, if we confess our sins, God will forgive us and cleanse us (see 1 John 1:9). After confessing our sins, we need to repent and turn away from all sins and from satan and his evil influences, and determine not to commit these sins again. We cannot confess our sins, repent, and then go back to those very sins again. If we do so, we will be going round in circles and will not be able to truly be delivered. We need to determine in our heart not to sin again, and we need to turn away from these sins, avoiding them and all circumstances that will tempt us to commit those sins again. We must guard ourselves and our lives and make every possible effort to turn our backs on the sins. The more we try and the more determined we are to break free, the sooner we will loose ourselves from the strongholds of sin that entangle us.

We need to forgive all other people who have wronged us and hurt us. For if we forgive others, God will also forgive us, but if we do not forgive others, God will also not forgive us (see Mark 11:25-26). Forgiveness is an act of our will; it has nothing to do with our emotions. We must will ourselves to forgive even if we do not feel like forgiving. It is a decision to choose to forgive others. We need to pray and ask God to deliver us and to set us free in the name of Jesus (see Joel 2:32). Finally, we need to use the weapons of submission to God, the blood of Jesus Christ, the Word of God, and our testimony as a believer, and wage warfare with the spiritual forces of darkness to release us from their holds.

After our deliverance, we must make every effort to retain our deliverance. We must guard ourselves, putting on the whole armor of God and standing firm in our faith. We must wear the belt of truth, the breastplate of righteousness, the shoes of peace, the shield of faith, the helmet of salvation, and the sword of the Spirit at all times (see Eph. 6:10-18). We must confess and believe in the Word of God, and it must be the light of our life that will expel all darkness and all lies. We must fill ourselves with the Word of God and use it to fight off the fiery arrows of the enemy and his attacks. Without the Word of God as our weapon, it is impossible for us to engage in this spiritual warfare. We must crucify the flesh and all old habits that are not in line with God and His righteousness and holiness. We must live holy lives. We must develop a lifestyle of continuous praise and prayer because praise silences the enemy, and we are commanded by God to pray without ceasing (see 1 Thess. 5:17). We must maintain a lifestyle of fellowship and accountability by being a member of a local church group and come together as one body, open and transparent to one another with our lifestyle. We must commit ourselves totally to Jesus Christ. We must submit to God and resist the devil, and he will flee from us (see James 4:7).

### ENDNOTE

1. Graham Cooke, *God Is the Kindest Person I Have Ever Met* (Teaching CD, 2005).

CHAPTER TEN

# Death, Where Is Thy Sting?

God does not keep a man *immune from trouble*; He says, "I will be with him in trouble."[1]

Oswald Chambers

*And it shall come to pass in the last days, saith God, I will pour out of My Spirit upon all flesh: and your sons and your daughters shall prophesy, and your young men shall see visions, and your old men shall dream dreams* (Acts 2:17).

## Tragedy Strikes Our Family

Two months after I discovered demons within me and less than one and a half years after I returned to Singapore, I was dealt another blow. My eldest

121

sister, who was only in her late 30's, died in a hotel room while on a holiday with my parents in Australia. It was an unexpected death that shocked our family. They had been having a good time in Australia, but on the last day of their tour, the day when they were expected to fly back to Singapore, my sister could not get out of bed. She complained that she was too tired and needed to rest. No one expected that this rest would mean that she would never wake up again.

## *Dying in Australia but Living in Eternity*

Before deciding which country to go to for a holiday, we had prayed and asked God, and we believed that Australia had been God's choice for our family. We never knew that it would be a journey that my sister would never return from.

However, God was aware of her coming death, and He divinely arranged for my family to be in touch with a Singaporean pastor who had moved to Australia. Throughout the time when my family was grieving, he, together with pastors of his church in Perth, supported and helped the family with all the funeral arrangements and with the task of bringing the body back from Australia to Singapore. They also extended their kindness by inviting my sister to stay at their home while waiting for the approvals to release the corpse. He and other pastors also ministered to my aging parents who grieved at having to say good-bye to their young daughter. Hence, for the first time in my father's life, he listened to the Gospel of Jesus Christ. Although my father continued to harden his heart and did not want to believe in Jesus Christ as his Lord and Savior, we were grateful to God for His mercy and for the opportunity for the Gospel to be shared.

My brother and I had stayed in Singapore while they were on their trip to Australia, and when I heard the news that my

eldest sister had passed away, I was shocked. It was a very sur-
prising and painful loss, especially because there had been no
physical signs or symptoms that she was soon going to die. I
was alone at home, crying out to God; I just could not understand why He had chosen to take her away from me.

Then I remembered that she had recently become a Christian, accepted Jesus Christ as her Lord and Savior, and started
going to church with us. Furthermore, a few weeks before the
family went to Australia, she admitted to me that she was
afraid that she would die in Australia. I told her that she
would not die but live (see Ezek. 18:21) and insisted that Jesus
Christ would save her no matter what happened. Should any
demon come and want to harm her, all she had to do was to cry
out, "Jesus Christ, save me," and if she couldn't speak with her
mouth, she could cry in her heart and God would hear her and
come and rescue her.

Then she told me of a recurrent dream she had been having. She had dreamt that a man in white holding a staff came
to her and told her that she would not die. Therefore, she
was assured, and I was also convinced that God had appeared to my sister and had comforted her, giving her assurance that she would not die.

And so, I left it as such and did not bother any more about
it. But when my eldest sister died, I remembered all these
things and realized that God in His foreknowledge had affirmed to both my sister and my family that she would not die
but live. She might have died physically, but she did not die
spiritually. She is with God for eternity. Indeed, she did not
die, but she lives in her spirit with God; and one day, I will see
her in Heaven. She will be part of a party who will welcome
me into the Kingdom of God. Indeed, death, where is your

sting? Death, where is your victory? (see 1 Cor. 15:55). The enemy can kill the body, but not the soul and the spirit of a man (see Matt. 10:28; 1 Cor. 5:4-5).

If any man believes in God, he will not perish but will have eternal life. For God did not send His Son into the world to condemn the world but that the world through Him might be saved. Whoever believes in Jesus Christ is not condemned, but whoever does not believe stands condemned already because he has not believed in the name of God's one and only Son (see John 3:16-18).

Indeed, I thank God that before my sister departed from this world, she believed in Jesus Christ and received Him into her life; therefore, she has eternal life, and we will unite again in Heaven one day. If you do not believe in Jesus Christ as Lord and Savior, won't you please make a decision this day and enter into the Kingdom of God right now and have eternal life. If you want to become a Christian, please see Appendix 2—How to Become a Christian.

## Dreams and Visions

Even though my eldest sister had accepted Jesus Christ as Lord and Savior before she passed away, I was still thrown into a state of confusion when she died. I still had questions. *Did she go to Heaven? Is she with God? She had not been baptized with water as was commanded by Jesus in the Bible, so is her salvation complete? Will she still go to Heaven, or is she banished to hell because she had not been baptized?*

One matter I am sure of—I do know that God is a God of love and a God of mercy. He is also a God of His Word, and His Word says that if anyone confesses with their mouth, "Jesus is Lord," and believes in their heart that God has raised Him from the dead, they will be saved (see Rom. 10:9). My sister was saved even though she had yet to be baptized by water.

However, anyone who has confessed their faith in Jesus Christ should be baptized. Nobody knows the full implication of water baptism, and only on the day of judgment, when we come before God face-to-face, will we understand the importance of this holy sacrament.

God in His mercy, knowing my confusion about what happened to my sister, showed us through dreams and visions that indeed my sister is with Him in paradise. Moreover, on the night that my sister passed away, one of my pastors visited me. While praying for me, she saw a vision of my sister sitting at a banqueting table laden with food and having a great time. She was really happy. My eldest sister had loved to eat when she was alive; indeed, food was a very important part of her life, and so this vision gave much comfort to me and affirmed that she is with God.

After my sister's death, my mother grieved very deeply. My mother had been sick for many years, and it was my eldest sister who took care of her. They were very close companions, and this loss was a big blow to her. The entire family was very worried about her emotional and mental well-being.

Then my mother began to have dreams about my dead sister, and in one of her dreams, she saw herself and my two sisters in a big boat. They all were dressed in white and were having a wonderful time. Indeed, everyone on that boat was dressed in white, and they were surrounded by beautiful scenery. The dream was very symbolic as my parents and two sisters had been on a cruise boat when they were in Australia. My sister had enjoyed this cruise very much, and it was one of her favorite parts of the tour. It was as though God was affirming to us that my sister is in Heaven, and one day, we all would be united once again. Interestingly, four of my family members had gone on the cruise in the physical, yet only three members appeared in the dream dressed in white. My father was missing in the dream. As of today, he still has not accepted Jesus Christ as his Lord and Savior. Please pray for him.

Subsequent to this dream, my mother had other dreams of my sister where she was always dressed in white and was always happy. In addition, during her lifetime on earth, my sister was rather plump; however, when my mother saw her in the dreams, she was very young in age, and her body was slim and lovely. Through the many dreams and visions of various people, God assured us of where our sister was—with Him in Heaven. My family was very comforted by the tenderness that the Lord was showing, and experienced the very words in Acts where God says that in the last days, the people will prophesy, see visions, and dream dreams.

## Financial Provision

During this overwhelmingly sad time, my family had to make preparations for my sister's funeral and burial. First, we had to arrange for her body to be flown back from Australia to Singapore. When the body reached Singapore, a funeral would be held, the body would be cremated, and the bones would be housed. All these events came and went, and then we had to contend with the practical financial aspects.

It had not been cheap for four people to go for a holiday to Australia. In addition, we had to pay to fly the body from Australia to Singapore and all the bills relating to the funeral. This amounted to a huge sum of money. My sister's death was sudden, and we had not purchased much insurance for her. Furthermore, because the cause of death was not known, we had to wait for the coroner's report before it could be determined whether the expenses could be claimed. But the bills still needed to be paid whether there would be any insurance payout or not. And when the credit card bill came, we were not sure where the money was going to come from to pay the expenses.

So, we prayed and asked God to provide the money to pay the bills. But the days came and went, and nothing happened. We had no other means of paying off the huge sum, except depending on God to provide. And God was faithful and did not fail us. On the day that the bills were due, we were given a sum of money that was more than enough to pay the full amount. Although we had been anxious and worried, God provided. We had been fearful and doubted whether God could provide what we needed at the time we needed it, and as the days went by, we almost gave up hope. But when we were faithless, God remained faithful (see 2 Tim. 2:13). He was faithful to my family, faithful to meet our needs, faithful to supply exceedingly, abundantly, and much more than we could ask or hope for.

Friends, if you have any needs—financial needs, physical needs, emotional needs—I ask that you do not give up. Do not give up trusting God to provide; do not give up praying and crying out to Him to come and rescue you. It might often seem that God does not hear, or He might appear to be late; but this is not true. He always hears every prayer, and in His time, He will come, in all His glory, in His entire splendor. We must rest in His nature, His character, His ways. He does not change like shifting shadows. He is a good God, a good Father who gives good gifts to His children.

## More Financial Provision

Three months after enduring our first financial trouble, we experienced another financial crisis. We had been using the money in my Central Provident Funds (CPF) savings account to pay for our housing loan. Since I had not been working full-time, the amount in my CPF had been steadily decreasing to a point where I had a zero balance in this account. And because the interest rate for my loan had increased from two percent to more than five percent per annum, the monthly housing payment amount had increased from $700 to almost $1000 a month. We once again needed God to intervene and come to our rescue.

Since I had returned to Singapore about one and half years before, in 2004, I had felt a burden to pay off the housing loan, and I continued to pray daily about this matter. God had provided when I attended the Discipleship Training School in Scotland, and He had also miraculously provided for all the debt relating to my sister's death. Now, once again, I needed God to provide for my needs. God had not failed me when I was in desperate need, and I knew He would not fail me now. So, we prayed for God to provide, even before the CPF account was completely bankrupt.

We know God has promised in His Word that we can test Him, and when we bring the whole tithe into the storehouse, there will be food in God's house. He will then open the floodgates of Heaven and pour out so much blessing that we will not have room enough for it (see Mal. 3:10). Both my sister and I had been faithful and consistent in giving our tithes to God. Without fail, month after month, no matter what financial situation we were in, we would give at least ten percent or more to the church as commanded in the Word of God (see Gen. 28:22). And through all the years as Christians, no matter how difficult it was financially or what crisis we faced, we had never lacked, because the hands of our Father had provided again and again, and we saw the faithfulness of God to us. There were many times we doubted Him, and our eyes could not see in the physical realm;

but God never failed to provide for our financial needs. Indeed, He had been very creative when providing financially through various means. In fact, we had never received financial provision in the same manner twice. It had always been different and always from an unexpected source. But it came—although sometimes much later than we would have liked. At times, finances come in natural ways, so normal that you tend to forget that it is from God; but when you reflect on the occasion, you can surely see God's hand and imprint on the provision, financial or otherwise.

So once again, we prayed and we waited. And once again, we received the needed money. The government of Singapore had established an insurance account for every Singaporean who had ever worked and contributed to a Central Provident Funds account with the Dependent Protection Scheme (DPS). The beneficiaries of anyone who died would receive a sum of money from this account. So after we informed the government of the death of our sister, we received a check from DPS a few months later, at the exact time when my CPF account had a zero balance. And it was enough to pay for our home loan for a few years. God had once again come through for us and our needs.

## Even More Financial Provision

As I mentioned previously, after I returned to Singapore, sometime in late 2004, I felt God impress upon my heart to pray for supernatural finance to pay off the entire housing loan. With what little faith that I had, I started to pray that God would provide the supernatural finance to pay off my entire housing loan within five years. At that point in time, it was an impossible and crazy dream. I had not received any finances "supernaturally," other than the amount I had received just before I went to attend DTS in Scotland. In addition, I had never won or received anything in my 30 years, except a small video recorder which cost about $200 when I was about 14 years old in a lucky draw. But I wanted to believe God, and so I just kept on praying for God to provide even though I could not see anything happen in the physical. Thereafter, we received money to pay off the funeral expenses in November 2005, and then received a second financial provision that came around April 2006 from the DPS to pay off the monthly HDB loan for a few years. We then received a third financial provision from an unexpected source, which completely paid off the entire housing loan.

Although we had not expected such a tragedy to happen to my family during their vacation, we had nevertheless purchased insurance for my family prior to their trip to Australia. And when the coroner's report was received after almost six months of waiting, it revealed that my sister had died of food poisoning. We then sent the bills to the insurance company in April 2006, and in the middle of May 2006, the insurance company called and informed us that we could claim only less than $10,000—the amount that had been approved and would be sent to management for endorsement before being disbursed to us.

Refusing to accept this outcome, my sister and I brought this issue before the Lord and continued to pray that there would be a breakthrough, so that that we could claim more than the insurance company had indicated. We heard nothing from the insurance company for almost two months, but we continued to pray. Then, on July 11, 2006, we received a phone call from the insurance company, stating that another claim amount had been approved. And it was a six-figure amount! We have no idea why the insurance company changed their minds, but we believe it was God's divine intervention. With this amount and the DPS amount we received in April 2006, we were able to completely cover the payment of the entire housing loan debt.

We learned that we must stop limiting God in His ways and learn to trust that He is good, even when we do not understand. Often, we do not notice God's financial gifts that are provided through what we consider to be everyday, normal means. But if we look closer and consider the timing of His provision, the amount and magnitude, and the extent of what happened, we can surely see God's fingerprints and His handiwork in our lives. I urge you to believe that God is a God of the supernatural. His name is Jehovah Jireh, the God who provides (see Gen. 12:13-14). Even while I did not have faith and could not believe, God showed Himself to be faithful, to be bigger than all my problems and all my worries (see 2 Tim. 2:13).

Depend on God and not on yourself. Pray until something happens. You might not see it immediately in the physical realm, but believe and keep on praying. Something happens in the spirit realm when we pray, and one day, you will see the answer in the physical realm (see Dan. 10:10-21).

I had little faith that we could pay off the entire housing loan by 2009; it was too much to expect from God. But He accomplished it by 2006—three years earlier than my expectation and less than two years after I had started to pray.

I have been praying for the salvation of my father ever since I became a Christian and have been now praying for more than 20 years, but I have yet to see him accept Christ. But I believe that in God's time, he will. I don't know why some prayers take more than 20 years, and others a few years or less; but one thing I know—when we pray, something happens. Sometimes we can see it when it happens, sometimes not. In any case, I urge you to go on praying, no matter what it is that you are praying for. Believe even when you do not see, because one day, God will open the windows of Heaven. He will turn a switch, and you will see your prayers answered, if it is prayed according to His will. Take up God's challenge—bring the whole tithe to His storehouse and test Him. He will not turn a deaf ear to His children who live by His Word (see Mal. 3:10). When He seems to be late, continue to be faithful. Continue to obey His commandments and walk according to His Word. Trust His heart and love for you, even when you cannot see His hand at work in your life. Be prepared for the unexpected. Be prepared for the pain and the tears, but also for the joy and the grace.

Indeed, God is Jehovah Jireh, the God who provides. He is our true provider. He can and He will provide for all our needs. The question is: Do we trust Him to provide? Or do we attempt to find other means and ways to meet our needs instead of going to God, pouring out to Him, and expecting Him to listen and to act on our behalf? It is not always so easy to trust God to provide, and there will be many heart-stopping moments. And as a Christian, what you do and how you choose to do things will often appear as foolishness in the eyes of the world. You will be ridiculed and laughed at, ostracized and looked down upon. Many people will misunderstand you, your intentions, and your heart. But press on, walk on, crawl on—soldier of the Lord Most High.

No matter what it takes to reach your destination, do not give up. If you must crawl, then do so. Let nothing stop you; let nothing move you. If you are struck down, pick yourself up again and continue. If fear assaults you, remind yourself of what God says—perfect love casts away all fear (see 1 John 4:18). God has not given you a spirit of fear, but of power, of love, and of a sound mind (see 2 Tim. 1:7). If you are disappointed and discouraged and there is no hope within you, cling to the Word of God. He is faithful. He will never leave you or forsake you (see

Heb. 13:5). You must learn to sense God beside you in the ebb and in the flow. For the message of the cross is foolishness to those who are perishing, but to us who are being saved, it is the power of God (see 1 Cor. 1:18).

We must never question in the dark (the difficult, trying moments of our life) what we have seen in the light (the provision, gifts, and mercies of God). In the dark periods of our lives, we must go to the recesses of our mind and pull forth those memories when God came through for us, when we received His financial help, physical healing, or when a prayer was answered. We must cling to these memories and trust that in whatever deep and dark situation we find ourselves right now, God will once again come through for us. He has not forgotten or forsaken us.

## ENDNOTE

1. Oswald Chambers, *My Utmost for His Highest* (Uhrichsville, OH: Babour Publishing, 1935).

## CHAPTER ELEVEN

# The Unknown Future

Holding On, Praying Expectantly (*H.O.P.E.*).

Author Unknown

*For I know the thoughts that I think toward you, saith the Lord, thoughts of peace, and not of evil, to give you an expected end* (Jeremiah 29:11).

## Jesus Is the Truth

Chapters One to Three of this book spanned 28 years of my life, whereas the events detailed in Chapters Four through Ten occurred during a span of less than two years. Unbelievable as it seems, what happened in less than two years totally changed the previous 28 years of my life and caused me to question more than 16 years of knowledge about the Bible acquired in a traditional church.

It has been an incredible journey thus far. It has not always been easy. In fact, many times, it has been difficult; and along the way, there have been many times when I wanted to give up, when I had no strength to walk on, no hope within me, no ounce of effort left to trust and believe God. But God has remained faithful to me, even when I was faithless. He has never given up on me, even when I ranted at Him and accused Him, when I shouted into His face and called Him a liar, when I refused to accept His love for me or accept the path He had chosen for me, when I refused to listen to His words of compassion and mercy, when I refused His help from unexpected places, and when I groped in the dark even though He was holding a light and standing in a corner waiting for me to come to Him. He was waiting to rescue me if I was only willing to let Him.

Perhaps many of you have been like me, refusing to see that God is real and that He can help. You might think that God helps only those who help themselves or helps those who are good enough or who have not sinned. You might be wondering and thinking, *Who am I? I am a nobody. God is not going to turn His eyes upon me and rescue me from the pit where I have fallen. I am too hopeless and helpless. No one can help me, not even God.*

But those are lies from the pit and from the mouth of the devil, the archenemy of man! He is lying to you so that you will end up like him, in the bottomless pit and in the lake of fire, so that you will suffer an end and eternity with him. Misery loves company, and the enemy wants you to join him in his misery. Please do not fall into the trap that the enemy has laid out for you. Please do not join him in the pit. You can make a decision right now. You can choose Jesus Christ right now and enter into eternal life. Your end does not have to be in the pit together with the devil. You do not need to suffer in shame and humiliation. You do not have to hang your head. Yes, you have sinned, sinned against God, against yourself, against your spouse, against your children, against your friends or business associates, against the people around you who love you and care for you. Indeed, the Bible says all men have sinned and fallen short of the glory of God (see Rom. 3:23). We all have sinned, some more than others, but sin is sin. Big or small, a sin is still a sin, and the wages of sin is death (see Rom. 6:23). Our end is death and the lake of fire, and no one can escape, because we live in a fallen world and we are a fallen people.

But God has prepared an alternative for us, and we ourselves can choose whether we want God's alternative or to suffer for eternity in hell. There is only one way. Jesus says, "I am the way and the truth and the life. No one comes to the Father except through Me" (John 14:6 NIV). No man can go to the Father, no man can receive eternal life except through Jesus Christ, the Lamb who was slain for the sins of the world. Jesus said that He came into the world to save those who are sick, to save sinners, and not those who are well and righteous (see Mark 2:17). Jesus came for sinners, not the righteous. He can raise the dead, He can command the winds and the waves, He can cast out demons, He can heal those who are sick, He can perform signs and wonders. And today, He gives each and everyone that same privilege to do as He has done. In fact, He said that His disciples would do greater things than He had done (see John 14:12). We have records of men and women who have done the very things that Jesus Christ did and even more. Men and women like John G. Lake, Kathryn Kulman, and Smith Wigglesworth have proven through their lives that every word that the Bible says is true.

Will you throw away the doubts, the shame, and the fear, and come before God, seeking forgiveness for your sins and receive God into your life as your Savior—to learn to walk a life of faith and trust, to believe in the Word of God and not in the present physical circumstances that you are in?

In the book *Experiencing God*, authors Blackaby and King mention that Jesus Christ is the Truth, and when He comes in, He can shatter the truth of your life. When the disciples were in the storm, their truth was that they were going to perish while Jesus was asleep. But the moment Jesus woke up, He who is the Truth rebuked the storm, and it became calm. When the widow's only son lie dead in the coffin, her truth was, "My son is dead." But when Jesus came, He who is the Truth touched the coffin, and the son became alive and was restored.

> "Never, ever determine the truth of a situation by looking at the circumstances. Don't evaluate your situation until you have heard from Jesus. He is the Truth of all your circumstances"[1]

## *Jesus Changed My Home and Family*

When I first became a Christian at the age of 13 years, the only people in my family who were believers were my brother and I. My parents and two older sisters were non-believers and continued to worship idols for many years. In the meantime, we prayed for their salvation and that they too would come to know Jesus Christ as their personal Lord and Savior.

Today, almost 20 years since I first confessed with my mouth and believed in my heart that Jesus is Lord, God has brought many changes to my family. The changes were not always instantaneous, but gradually over time, they have been significant. I continued to live day-to-day by faith and trusting God even though many times, I was not able to see significant and miraculous things happen.

However, by God's grace, when we moved to our new home about two years ago, all the idols and graven images were not brought into our home. Despite much opposition by my father who is still an idol worshipper, God fought a spiritual war for us and made it possible for us to discard all the idols that had been in our family for more than three decades.

After almost twenty years of prayers, my mother and my two sisters were also converted to Christianity. My mother's schizophrenic condition has stabilized, and she has not been admitted to the Institute of Mental Health (IMH) for more than a decade. We believe God for her full and total recovery. My eldest sister accepted Christ as her Lord and Savior in 2004 before she passed away and went to be with the Lord on November 2, 2005. And although my father is not a believer yet, he has mellowed a lot since the early years and is more receptive to Christians. The quarrelling and his womanizing ways have ceased. Many other extended members of our family have also come to know Jesus Christ and profess Him as their personal Savior.

My family has never lacked in anything, and time and time again God has provided for all our needs. We have always been able to pay off all expenses for our family. And interestingly, these finances have often come in the most natural ways, but their timely arrival and amount speaks of a bigger entity who has orchestrated their coming. We believe that our provision has been given to us supernaturally by Almighty God.

Although we are grateful for all the mercies God has bestowed upon our family all these years, we still carry a huge burden for the salvation of our father. My family is praying for our father, and we claim and believe in God's promise in Acts

16 that when one in the house is saved, the whole house will be saved. We know that one day, he too will confess with his mouth and believe in his heart that Jesus Christ is Lord! And that one day, together with my deceased sister, we will be together again in Heaven and spend eternity with Christ.

## A Hope and a Future

I am holding on to God's hand and praying expectantly with regards to my future. I do not know what lies ahead or what I will face, but after the tremendous journey I have taken in the past two years, I know and believe that all things are possible. God is in control, and He is in charge. The future may be unknown to me, but it is known to God. The way ahead might seem dark and sinister, but I know who holds my hand and I am safe in my Father's care. In those times when I see only one pair of footprints in the sand, I know that these are the times when I can no longer walk and my Father is carrying me. I know that during the days ahead of me, even when I cannot see Him, He is beside me. His Word is true, and I hold on to His promise that He will never leave me or forsake me (see Heb. 13:5). In those times of deepest pain and loneliness, I hold on to the truth of His Word, His love letter, the Bible, that He has left behind to teach me all things.

Our walk as Christians is a journey—a journey to the heart of God and a walk of faith. I pray that like me, you too can face the future and walk on, no matter what kind of circumstances you are facing at this point in time on your journey. Know that God is always beside you and taking care of you. Look back to your own life, look back into the journey that you have taken since the day you accepted Jesus Christ as your Lord and Savior and realize the mercies that have been littered on the pathway of your life. You will not help but notice the hand of

God in your own life. What might have appeared to be normal circumstances was actually the distinct hand of God, although perhaps subtle and silent.

Do you see His hand? Do you see His touch in your life? Do you see His mercy and grace? He is there. He has watched over you and has taken care of you. Look back over the months, the seasons, and the years of your life, and I am sure, like me, you too will see and understand that God's marvelous hands have been at work.

He has walked with me even during the darkest and most painful period of my life, even when I felt that He had abandoned me, forgotten me, and neglected my existence. There were times when I felt He did not love me or care about me, when He was completely ignoring me. But how wrong I was! When I took the time to sit down and reflect upon my life and saw the changes that had been achieved, I clearly saw God's presence had always been with me. Things that I never thought were possible became a reality.

So, let us run the race and reach out for the prize that is in Christ Jesus our Lord (see Heb. 12:1-3; 1 Cor. 9:23-24). He never fails! Our future is safe in His hands because He knows the plans He has for us—plans to prosper us and not to harm us, plans to give us a hope and a future! (see Jer. 29:11).

## ENDNOTE

1. Henry T. Blackaby and Claude V. King, *Experiencing God* (Nashville, TN: Broadman & Holman Publishers, 2004), 194-195.

## CHAPTER TWELVE

# Pray Until Something Happens (P.U.S.H.)

To trust in spite of the look of being forsaken...and yet believe that God is awake and utterly loving...to wait patiently...such is the *victory* that overcometh the world, such is faith indeed.[1]

Mrs. Charles E. Cowman

*If ye abide in Me, and My words abide in you, ye shall ask what ye will, and it shall be done unto you* (John 15:7).

## Prayer—An Uphill Climb

Shortly after I returned to Singapore, I went to Malaysia with my brother and his students to trek a 500 meter-high mountain. As I climbed, I felt like

143

giving up. My brother and his students were going at such a fast pace, and I could not keep up. There were so many steep hills, and my legs were tired and very heavy. I had not exercised for four months, and I knew I was slowing the group down. Any group can only be as fast as the slowest man, and at one point, I seriously considered stopping and even turning back.

Then I felt God speak to me about the parallel between trekking a mountain and prayer. A man climbing is like a man praying, and the summit of a mountain symbolizes an answered prayer. Every step or trek you make forward is the same as every prayer prayed. It brings you a little closer to the summit. But when you stop trekking or praying, you come to a standstill. You are not moving towards the destination or summit; you are not getting any nearer to seeing your prayers answered.

However, you must continue to move forward no matter if you are too tired, or it is too difficult, or your legs hurt—no matter what. You must keep on praying, even when you don't feel like it, even when you feel discouraged or disappointed, or when the answer to a prayer does not come after a long time. If you turn back, you won't reach the summit. Giving up means that all your previous trekking or praying has been in vain, because now you are moving away from the summit of answered prayer. However, if you move forward, keep on trekking or praying, no matter how difficult it is, how much your legs hurt, how much you want to give up, how silent God seems, *sooner or later, you will reach the summit. You will see your prayers answered.*

You must persevere in spite of the difficulties and uncertainties. Every step, trek, or prayer brings you a little closer to the summit. Don't give up, don't lose hope. Keep on pushing forward.

## *Don't Give Up—Press On!*

When we finally reached the summit, my brother informed us that we had accomplished the climb 25 minutes faster than an earlier team he had brought there. And I had been thinking that I was holding the group back and we were going much slower than we should have been. The reality was I had been deceived even in the midst of the trek, and only when I reached the summit did I realize the truth.

It is the same when praying. We might feel that we are not moving ahead, and it is a slow and painful process; but when the prayer is answered, we can see that we had been going forward all along. God had been moving, and indeed, things had changed.

I believe God wants to speak to some of us about prayers and to others about the Christian walk. Climbing a mountain is also like being a Christian walking with God. Some of us might have started the climb, but midway through, we gave up. We stopped going forward, or worse, some of us turned around and started going downhill because the journey upward was too difficult. We had not received what we believed when we first became Christians. We became discouraged and couldn't bring our legs to go on.

But Jesus is always waiting for us at the summit. We need to go through the pain and the strain so that our muscles can work and grow strong, so that we can be built into strong men and women of God. The process is as important as the destination. An athlete will never win the prize if he doesn't go through training and strain his muscles through various physical challenges. A diver will never be able to see the wonders of the depths if he does not first learn how to use the equipment and put himself in the dangerous environment of the deep sea. A violin will never be able to produce beautiful music if its strings are not put through the strain but are merely left alone. A candle will never be able to give light if it is not burned and its wax not melted.

May we all learn to go on, even when everything within us says we cannot, even when it seems too difficult, when we can't see what is ahead, when we are tired, or we think it is useless. Giving up is an easy choice to make, while going on when everything seems against you and when God seems to remain silent is much more difficult. May we hold on to God and His promises, believing that He is in control at all times. Remember that our momentary, small problems are producing in us an eternal reward, which we will receive if we do not give up.

I urge you to P.U.S.H—pray until something happens. Push onward and forward, and believe that God is faithful, that He will never leave you or forsake you even when circumstances are adverse and it seems He has abandoned you. Beloved, you must not believe in the lies of the enemy. You must not trust in what you can see with your physical eyes. Rather, you must put your trust and your faith in the unseen God because what is seen is temporary and what is unseen is eternal. Hold on to the goodness, the faithfulness, the love, the mercy, the compassion of God our heavenly Father. Cry out to Him in desperation. Cry out and keep on crying until He hears your voice, until He comes down and scoops you up, until He comes and hides you under the shelter of His mighty wings. Let nothing move you. Look forward to the destiny that He has for you. Look back at those times when He turned up in your life. If He did it then, He will do it now. Wait…wait for Him to come, because those who wait upon the Lord will renew their strength, they will mount on wings of eagles, they will run and not be weary, they will walk on and not grow faint (see Isa. 40:31).

## ENDNOTE

1. Mrs. Charles E. Cowman, *Streams in the Desert and Springs in the Valley* (Grand Rapids, MI: Zondervan Publishing House, 1996).

# Appendix 1

# APPENDIX 1

# Basics About the Holy Spirit

## Who Is the Holy Spirit?

1. He is a person.

   *And I will ask the Father, and He will give you another Counselor to be with you forever* (John 14:16 NIV).

2. He is God.

   *Now the earth was formless and empty, darkness was over the surface of the deep, and the **Spirit of God** was hovering over the waters* (Genesis 1:2 NIV, emphasis added).

   *Then God said, "**Let Us** make man in Our image, in Our likeness, and let them rule over the fish of the sea and the birds of the air, over the livestock, over all the earth, and over all the creatures that move along the ground"* (Genesis 1:26 NIV, emphasis added).

*Therefore go and make disciples of all nations, baptizing them in the name of the **Father** and of the **Son** and of the **Holy Spirit*** (Matthew 28:19 NIV, emphasis added).

*Again **Jesus** said, "Peace be with you! As the **Father** has sent Me, I am sending you." And with that He breathed on them and said, "Receive the **Holy Spirit"*** (John 20:21-22 NIV, emphasis added).

3. He gives life.

*Jesus answered, "I tell you the truth, no one can enter the kingdom of God unless he is born of water and the Spirit. Flesh gives birth to flesh, but the Spirit gives birth to spirit* (John 3:5-6 NIV).

*The Spirit gives life; the flesh counts for nothing* (John 6:63a NIV).

4. He is the God who lives in you.

*Don't you know that you yourselves are God's temple and that God's Spirit lives in you?* (1 Corinthians 3:16 NIV).

*Do you not know that your body is a temple of the Holy Spirit, who is in you, whom you have received from God?...* (1 Corinthians 6:19 NIV).

## What Is the Baptism of the Holy Spirit?

1. The baptism of the Holy Spirit means "to be immersed and covered and flooded with the light and revelation of the Holy Spirit, the third person of the Trinity, that your whole body will be filled, and not only filled but also covered until you walk in the presence of the power of God"[1] It is the inward filling of the Holy Spirit that results in outward signs like speaking in tongues.

[Jesus said,] *"If anyone is thirsty, let him come to Me and drink. Whoever believes in Me, as the Scripture has said, streams of living water will flow from within him." By this He meant the Spirit, whom those who believed in Him were later to receive. Up to that time the Spirit had not been given, since Jesus had not yet been glorified* (John 7:37b-39 NIV).

2. Fulfillment of Joel's prophecy. The baptism of the Holy Spirit is for all believers.

   *And afterward, I will pour out My Spirit on all people. Your sons and daughters will prophesy, your old men will dream dreams, your young men will see visions. Even on My servants, both men and women, I will pour out My Spirit in those days* (Joel 2:28-29 NIV).

3. Fulfillment of Jesus' promise. Joel's prophecy was confirmed by Jesus and was fulfilled at Pentecost, and even in this day 2000 years later, many of God's people are baptized with the Holy Spirit and receive dreams and visions.

   [Jesus said,] *"Do not leave Jerusalem, but wait for the gift My Father promised, which you have heard Me speak about. For John baptized with water, but in a few days you will be baptized with the Holy Spirit"* (Acts 1:4b-5 NIV).

   *They saw what seemed to be tongues of fire that separated and came to rest on each of them. All of them were filled with the Holy Spirit and began to speak in other tongues as the Spirit enabled them* (Acts 2:3-4 NIV).

# How Do I Receive the Baptism of the Holy Spirit?

1. Baptism of the Holy Spirit is sent by Jesus to believers.

   [Jesus said,] *"But I tell you the truth: It is for your good that I am going away. Unless I go away, the Counselor will not come to you; but if I go, I will send Him to you"* (John 16:7 NIV).

   *And with that, He [Jesus] breathed on them and said, "Receive the Holy Spirit"* (John 20:22 NIV).

2. Laying on of hands by other disciples who have already received the Holy Spirit.

   *When the apostles in Jerusalem heard that Samaria had accepted the word of God, they sent Peter and John to them. When they arrived, they prayed for them that they might receive the Holy Spirit, because the Holy Spirit had not yet come upon any of them; they had simply been baptized into the name of the Lord Jesus. Then Peter and John placed their hands on them, and they received the Holy Spirit* (Acts 8:14-17 NIV).

   *On hearing this, they were baptized into the name of the Lord Jesus. When Paul placed his hands on them, the Holy Spirit came on them, and they spoke in tongues and prophesied* (Acts 19:5-6 NIV).

3. Anointing.

   *Then Samuel took a flask of oil and poured it on Saul's head and kissed him, saying "...The Spirit of the Lord will come upon you in power, and you will prophesy with them..."* (1 Samuel 10:1,6 NIV).

*Then the Lord said, "Rise and anoint him; he is the one."*
*So Samuel took the horn of oil and anointed him in the*
*presence of his brothers, and from that day on the Spirit*
*of the Lord came upon David in power...* (1 Samuel
16:12b-13 NIV).

4.  Repent and be baptized to receive the gift of the Holy
    Spirit.

*When the people heard this, they were cut to the heart and*
*said to Peter and the other apostles, "Brothers, what shall*
*we do?" Peter replied, "Repent and be baptized, every one*
*of you, in the name of Jesus Christ for the forgiveness of*
*your sins. And you will receive the gift of the Holy Spirit*
(Acts 2:37-38 NIV).

5.  Coming of the Holy Spirit.

*They saw what seemed to be tongues of fire that separated*
*and came to rest on each of them. All of them were filled*
*with the Holy Spirit and began to speak in other tongues*
*as the Spirit enabled them* (Acts 2:3-4 NIV).

6.  Be thirsty, believe, and drink.

*On the last and greatest day of the Feast, Jesus stood*
*and said in a loud voice, "If anyone is thirsty, let him*
*come to Me and drink. Whoever believes in Me, as the*
*Scripture has said, streams of living water will flow*
*from within him." By this He meant the Spirit, whom*
*those who believed in Him were later to receive. Up to*
*that time the Spirit had not been given, since Jesus had*
*not yet been glorified* (John 7:37-39 NIV).

7.  Ask God.

*You want something but don't get it. You kill and covet, but you cannot have what you want. You quarrel and fight. You do not have, because you do not ask God* (James 4:2 NIV).

*If you then, though you are evil, know how to give good gifts to your children, how much more will your Father in heaven give the Holy Spirit to those who ask Him!* (Luke 11:13 NIV).

## How Do I Know I Have Been Baptized by the Holy Spirit?

1. Speaking in tongues.

*All of them were filled with the Holy Spirit and began to speak in other tongues as the Spirit enabled them* (Acts 2:4 NIV).

*While Peter was still speaking these words, the Holy Spirit came on all who heard the message. The circumcised believers who had come with Peter were astonished that the gift of the Holy Spirit had been poured out even on the Gentiles. For they heard them speaking in tongues and praising God* (Acts 10:44-46 NIV).

*When Paul placed his hands on them, the Holy Spirit came on them, and they spoke in tongues and prophesied* (Acts 19:6 NIV).

2. Manifestation of the gifts of the Holy Spirit.

*Now to each one the manifestation of the Spirit is given for the common good. To one there is given through the Spirit the message of wisdom, to another the message of knowledge by means of the same Spirit, to another faith by the same Spirit, to another gifts of healing by that one Spirit, to another miraculous powers, to another prophecy, to another distinguishing between spirits, to another speaking in different kinds of tongues, and to still another the interpretation of tongues. All these are the work of one and the same Spirit, and He gives them to each one, just as He determines* (1 Corinthians 12:7-11 NIV).

3.  Dreams and visions.

*And afterward, I will pour out My Spirit on all people. Your sons and daughters will prophesy, your old men will dream dreams, your young men will see visions. Even on My servants, both men and women, I will pour out My Spirit in those days* (Joel 2:28-29 NIV).

## ENDNOTE

1.  Smith Wigglesworth, *On the Holy Spirit* (New Kensington, PA: Whitaker House, 1988), 21.

# Appendix 2

# How to Become a Christian

| Man | God |
|-----|-----|

Death
Judgment

**SIN**

## Man Has Sinned and Is Separated From God

*For all have sinned and fall short of the glory of God* (Romans 3:23 NIV).

*For the wages of sin is death, but the gift of God is eternal life in Christ Jesus our Lord* (Romans 6:23 NIV).

*Just as man is destined to die once, and after that to face judgment* (Hebrews 9:27 NIV).

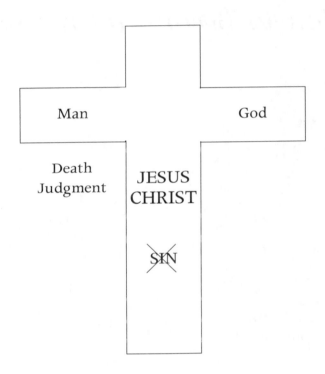

## Christ Died for Us, While We Were Yet Sinners

*For God so loved the world that He gave His one and only Son, that whoever believes in Him shall not perish but have eternal life* (John 3:16 NIV).

*But God demonstrates His own love for us in this: While we were still sinners, Christ died for us* (Romans 5:8 NIV).

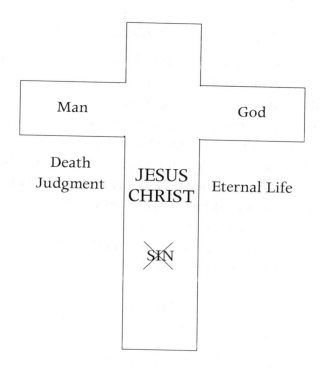

## The Gift of God Is Eternal Life

*I tell you the truth, whoever hears My* [Christ's] *word and believes Him who sent Me* [Christ] *has eternal life and will not be condemned; he has crossed over from death to life* (John 5:24 NIV).

*That if you confess with your mouth, "Jesus is Lord," and believe in your heart that God raised Him from the dead, you will be saved. For it is with your heart that you believe and are justified, and it is with your mouth that you confess and are saved* (Romans 10:9-10 NIV).

*For it is by grace you have been saved, through faith— and this not from yourselves, it is the gift of God—not by works, so that no one can boast* (Ephesians 2:8-9 NIV).

## Prayer to Become a Christian

Dear God, I know that Jesus Christ died on the cross for my sin. Please forgive me of my sins; I want to come back to You. I acknowledge that I am a sinner, and I repent of my wrongdoings. I believe that Jesus died for me, and I accept and invite Jesus into my life as my personal Lord and Savior. You said in Your Word that if I confess with my mouth, "Jesus is Lord," and believe in my heart that God has raised Him from the dead, I will be saved. With my confession and my belief, I now enter into the Kingdom of God and become a child of God. In Jesus' name I pray. Amen.

## Congratulations! You Are Now a Child of God

Congratulations! Praying these words and meaning them with your heart and mind, you have now become a son or daughter of God. Yes, it is that easy. You might or might not feel anything; but God has come into your life, and your life will be transformed. You need to find a local church where you can have fellowship with other brothers and sisters in Christ. It is the start of a journey, and who knows—you might soon be writing a story about your own life and adventures with God!

*Glossary*

# Glossary

**Charismatic churches**   For the purpose of this book, this term is used loosely to describe churches that believe in the Holy Spirit and move in the gifts of the Holy Spirit, such as speaking in tongues and prophecy.

**CPF**   Central Provident Fund is a unique compulsory savings plan in Singapore. Each month, every person who works in Singapore contributes between 20 to 40 percent of his monthly salary to this savings account.

**DTS**   Discipleship Training School.

| | |
|---|---|
| *Ghost Festival* | An annual month-long event during which the Chinese believe that the souls are released from hell and allowed to roam on earth for a month. Tents are set up all over Singapore and performances are held. Auctions are held to sell off religious idolatry items, such as statues of gods and storage items with words of blessings written on them. |
| *Guan Yin* | Chinese name for "Goddess of Mercy," an idol worshipped by the Chinese. |
| *HDB* | Housing Development Board, an institution that builds flats for Singaporeans. |
| *Mahjong* | A Chinese game in which players choose and place small painted pieces of wood or other material on a square table, attempting to gain the correct combination in order to win. |
| *Monkey gods* | Humans who are associated with a Chinese temple. They are mediums who invite "gods" or "unclean spirits" to come into their body and use their body for rituals or for fortune-telling. Superstitious people approach them to ask about their own |

future, marriage, or other personal matters. They also perform feats, such as eating fire and lifting extremely heavy weights.

**Nitrogen narcosis**

A diving condition in which nitrogen has a progressive narcotic effect on a person at depths more than 30 meters. It can make the diver less able to cope with problems.

**Qing Ming**

An annual festival where the dead are remembered. Members of households burn paper money, paper houses, paper items, and joss sticks, believing that once burned, these will be received by the dead in hell. During this festival, people also go to graveyards and crematoriums where bones are buried, to pay respect to the dead by burning joss sticks.

**Traditional churches**

For the purpose of this book, this term is used loosely to describe churches that believe in the Holy Spirit but do not move in the gifts of the Holy Spirit, such as speaking in tongues and prophecy.

**YWAM**

Youth With a Mission.

# Bibliography

Blackaby, Henry T. and King, Claude V. *Experiencing God* (Nashville, TN: Broadman & Holman Publishers, 2004).

Bright, Bill. *The Greatest Lesson I've Ever Learned: For Men* (Orlando, FL: New Life Publication, 2000).

Chambers, Oswald. *My Utmost for His Highest* (Uhrichsville, OH: Babour Publishing, 1935).

Cooke, Graham. *When the Lights Go Out* (Grand Rapids, MI: Chosen, 2003).

Cowman, Mrs. Charles E. *Streams in the Desert and Springs in the Valley* (Grand Rapids, MI: Zondervan Publishing House, 1996).

Curtis, Brent and Eldredge, John. *The Sacred Romance* (Nashville, TN: Thomas Nelson, 1997).

Doctorian, Samuel. *My Daily Strength* (Jakarta, ID: Immanuel Publishing House).

Goll, Jim W. *The Beginner's Guide to Hearing God* (Ventura, CA: Regal, 2004).

Hammond, Frank and Ida Mae. *Pigs in the Parlor* (Kirkwood, MO: Impact Christian Books, 1973).

Johnson, Bill. *The Supernatural Power of a Transformed Mind* (Shippensburg, PA: Destiny Image Publishers, 2006).

McClung, Floyd. *Spirits of the City* (Eastbourne UK: Kingsway Communications, 1990).

Prince, Derek. *Blessing or Curse: You Can Choose* (Christchurch, NZ: Derek Prince Ministries, 1990).

*They Shall Expel Demons* (Grand Rapids, MI: Chosen Books, 1998).

Sherman, Dean. *Spiritual Warfare for Every Christian* Study Guide Edition (Seattle, WA: YWAM Publishing, 1995).

Tenny, Tommy. *The God Chasers* (Shippensburg, PA: Destiny Image Publishers, 1998).

Wigglesworth, Smith. *On the Holy Spirit* (New Kensington, PA: Whitaker House, 1998).

# Recommended Reading

Cooke, Graham. *Developing Your Prophetic Gifting* (Grand Rapids, MI: Chosen, 2000).

Cunningham, Loren. *Daring to Live on the Edge* (Seattle, WA: YWAM Publishing, 1992).

*Is That Really You, God? Hearing the Voice of God* (Seattle, WA: YWAM Publishing 2001).

Deere, Jack. *Surprised by the Power of the Spirit* (Grand Rapids, MI: Zondervan Publishing House, 1993).

*The Beginner's Guide to the Gift of Prophecy* (Ventura, CA: Regal Books, 2001).

Dueck, Murray. *If This Were a Dream, What Would It Mean?* (Abbotsford, BC, Canada: Fresh Wind Press, 2006).

Hamon, Bill. *Prophets and the Prophetic Movement* (Shippensburg, PA: Destiny Image Publishers, 1990).

Hamon, Jane. *Dreams and Visions* (Ventura, CA: Regal, 2000).

Pierce, Chuck D. and Wagner Sytsema, Rebecca. *Prayers That Outwit the Enemy* (Ventura, CA: Regal, 2004).

*When God Speaks* (Colorado Springs, CO: Wagner Publications, 2003).

Piper, Don. *90 Minutes in Heaven* (Grand Rapids, MI: Revell, 2004).

Prince, Derek. *The Holy Spirit in You* (New Kensington, PA: Whitaker House, 1987).

*The Power of Proclamation* (Christchurch, NZ: Derek Prince Ministries, 2002).

Sheets, Dutch. *Intercessory Prayer* (Ventura, CA: Regal Books, 1996).

Wentroble, Barbara. *Prophetic Intercession* (Ventura, CA: Regal, 1999).

Yun, Brother. *The Heavenly Man* (Mill Hill, London: Monarch Books, 2002).

# A new exciting title from DESTINY IMAGE EUROPE

## WHEN GOD SMILES

*By Ernest J. Cowper-Smith*

❖ Do you seem to be stumbling into snares and roadblocks every time you try to receive God's blessings and promises?

❖ Do you receive financial blessings only to find they disappear as if you have holes in your pockets?

❖ Do you keep falling into the same trap over and over again?

❖ Do you ever feel that God is punishing you and you don't understand why?

❖ Are you having difficulty being set free from harmful habits or sinful obsessions, or granting forgiveness?

Receiving God's promises often requires more than faith, more than confession, and more than a head knowledge of those promises. Moreover, the enemy of our souls uses schemes to prevent God's children from fulfilling their destiny and calling in life.

For these reasons, Ernest Cowper-Smith, having an in-depth knowledge of God's Word combined with his personal experience of life's trials and tribulations, explains how to overcome some of life's most painful predicaments in his book, *When God Smiles.*

Learn how not to be afraid of the trials and fiery ordeals you find yourself in, but to use them as stepping-stones to freedom, not stumbling blocks to your faith!

ISBN-13: 978-88-89127-56-8

## Order Now from Destiny Image Europe
Telephone: +39 085 4716623 - Fax +39 085 4716622
E-mail: ordini@eurodestinyimage.com

## Internet: www.eurodestinyimage.com

Additional copies of this book and other book
titles from DESTINY IMAGE EUROPE
are available at your local bookstore.

We are adding new titles every month!

To view our complete catalog online, visit us at:
**www.eurodestinyimage.com**

Send a request for a catalog to:

**Via Acquacorrente, 6
65123 - Pescara - ITALY
Tel. +39 085 4716623 - Fax +39 085 4716622**

*"Changing the world, one book at a time."*

---

Are you an author?

Do you have a "today" God-given message?

## CONTACT US

We will be happy to review your manuscript
for a possible publishing:

**publisher@eurodestinyimage.com**